W9-AFQ-551

What makes a woman GIB*

*good in bed

What makes a woman G.I.B.*

*good in bed

by Wendy Leigh

PENTHOUSE PRESS, LTD.
New York, N.Y.

Book trade distribution by Whirlwind Book Company

Cover design by SADIQ/MARRERO

Library of Congress Catalog Card No. 76-54370
ISBN No. 0-89110-012-1

Printed in the United States of America

First Edition

This book is dedicated to all other adventuresses:

To my grandmother, Gaggy, *who survived because of her dreams*

To my mother, Marion, *who still dreams and always will*

To my adopted sister, Jane, *who helped me, shared them with me, and is living out her own*

To Rebecca *and* Debra, *who are young and still have dreams to find and the chance to live them*

To the memory of Maria, *who has no more chances or dreams, but who gave me mine*

To every woman who has ever tried to live out her fantasies and her dreams and who has believed in herself.

We should ask for no absolutes or absolute. Once and for all and forever let us have done with ugly imperialism of any absolute. There is no absolute good. There is nothing absolutely right. All things flow and change, and even change is not absolute.

D. H. LAWRENCE, *Phoenix I.*

Contents

Part II: The Celebrities *(continued)*

Part II: The Celebrities *(continued)*

The Inside Story on GIB*

*good in bed

Warren Beatty shocked me. The setting was beautiful—a reception for Muhammad Ali at the Beverly Wilshire Hotel, Beverly Hills—but the memories it evoked certainly were not. The Beverly Wilshire will always remind me of my first month in California, the El Padrino Bar and middle-aged married men trying to make me, trying to persuade me, to leave the dark corner booths for the more spacious suites upstairs.

Most of all, the Wilshire will always remind me of the vice-president of a top Hollywood agency who took me to dinner there and told me, "Unless you go to bed with me, I won't allow you to interview any of our clients"—instantly confronting me with the truth of everything I had ever read about Hollywood.

Just as everything I had read about Hollywood was true, everything I had read about Warren Beatty certainly was not, as I discovered at that reception where Warren—very suntanned in a white suit — appeared intent on avoiding all but a select few.

Eventually I managed to catch his eye and ask him my question: "What makes a woman good in bed?" Warren Beatty, world-renowned idol and sex symbol, stared at me for a moment in outrage, and then replied, "What makes a woman good in bed? I think that is a terrible question,'' and walked off. I was shocked because that reply was unexpected coming from a sex symbol like Warren Beatty. But I was also pleased because I totally agree with him. I have always thought that the question, ''Are you good in bed?'' is terrible because of the insecurity and desire for sexual conformity it creates in women.

I was first confronted by the discovery that a sexual *good* existed in people's minds when I was sixteen and a friend sent me a card that read: ''To a little girl who was born good, but who is getting better and better with experience.'' When she explained what the card meant, I suddenly realized that my major sexual dilemma, whether or not to ''go all the way,'' was outdated because instead of worrying about ''going all the way,'' women were now worrying about what to do once they got ''there.'' Sexual liberation and the Pill had altered relationships; it used to be enough for a woman to say yes. Now she was not only *expected* to say yes, but also to be *good.*

I decided that, since this new sexual ingredient called *good* apparently existed, I wanted to *be* it, except that I didn't know what *good* was and no one seemed to be able to enlighten me. But as I was still a virgin, I expected the mysteries of *good* to be revealed when I finally went all the way. The glow of my first sexual experience totally obliterated the question of *good*—until the man unwittingly revived it by saying that I was ''very good,'' so unleashing upon himself three years of speculation on the theme of *good*. ''Why was I *good*?'' ''Would every man think I was *good*?'' ''What could I do to be *better*?'' ''How could I recognize *better* when I struck it?'' ''What if I developed a sudden case of *bad*?'' ''What if I deteriorated to *worse*?'' To all that he merely replied, ''Just be thankful that you *are* good.''

But I *wasn't* thankful, because I wanted to know more.

After many interviews with women, I wanted to know more. Later I found that other women had also attempted to discover what the criteria were for judging *good*. Was it face? figure? words? staying power? speed and ability to attain orgasm? secret sexual techniques? prowess at oral sex? Did *good* even exist? Few women knew, but many wanted to find out, not just out of curiosity, but primarily because *good* acquired monumental importance in their moments of deepest sexual insecurity: moments when they wondered if they were, or ever could be, *good*; moments when their relationships failed and they wondered if being *bad* had activated their failure; moments when they tried to be *good*, at the cost of their own pleasure, because they failed to ask for what they wanted in bed, or failed to refuse what they didn't want. And even without those insecurities, women were continually aware that the men who looked at them no longer thought, "Does she or doesn't she" (go to bed)? but, "Is she or isn't she" (*good* in bed)?

Occasionally men asked me the question, "Are you good in bed?" and I answered, "What *makes* a woman good in bed?" Each man would attempt a reply which contradicted every other reply I had previously received. The conflicting responses exploded any stereotypes or assumptions I had that sex is governed by any rules or rating systems. Each individual's answer diminished the importance and validity of good—and with it some of my sexual insecurities. But others still remained, along with a slight suspicion that there might perhaps somewhere still exist a formula for the "*perfect* woman in bed." I hoped none existed—but wanted to discover the truth—to resolve the entire issue for myself and for other women to whom I had spoken. Finally I decided to ask the world my question, and launched myself on an investigation which took me to London, New York, Las Vegas, and Los Angeles and resulted in this book.

First I interviewed medical professionals. I asked them questions such as: Is there a superior cunt? Can a gynecologist tell if a woman is *good* when he examines her? Does each woman have a fixed time span before she has an orgasm, and does the woman who is *good* have an orgasm more quickly? Do some vaginas taste *better* than others?

Then I interviewed male celebrities, the sex symbols universally desired by women. I asked them how a man who can sleep with almost any woman picks the one he wants. Can he tell by looking at the woman if she is *good*? Is the woman who is *good* always *good* the first time she goes to bed with a man? Does beauty make a woman *good* in bed? If they had the power to create the perfect woman in bed, what would she be like? Is a woman less *good* if she takes a long time to come? Is a woman born *good*? Is there a physical type or age group most likely to be *good* in bed? Does the woman who is *good* ever refuse anything in bed? Is a woman less *good* if she asks for what she wants? Does love add or detract from *good* sex? Does the woman who is *good* talk in bed? Finally, I asked them to describe the woman who is *bad* in bed.

Next I talked to the female celebrities, women envied throughout the world. I asked them what advice they would give to other women who want to be *good*. How can a woman project that she is *good*? Have *they* ever worried about being *good*? Have men ever made them feel sexually inadequate? Do they feel less *good* if they take a long time to come? Are they ever scared to ask for what they want in bed? Is there anything they would refuse in bed? Does the woman who is *good* change with each man she is in bed with? Are they equally *good* with all men? Have they ever faked in bed?

There were racy revelations from many celebrities, like the femme fatale who admits that she fakes in bed, and tells how; the singer who enjoys having a teenager in bed; the celebrity who explains how she masturbates with a water hose; the movie star who says a woman should be a slave in bed; the sex bomb who reveals that she dislikes being given head; the superstar who once counted a woman's fifty orgasms during a ten-hour love session.

For the next section, I interviewed the glamor professionals, men and women whose professions create an aura of sexuality around them, providing opportunities for countless sexual experiences, experiments, and judgments. I asked them how rare the woman is who is *good*. Is it difficult to be *good* in bed? Can a woman learn to be *good*? Does a bisexual experience teach a woman to be *good*? What is the difference between a man's opinion of what makes a woman *good* in bed and her own? Can a woman be non-orgasmic yet still be *good*? Do all women who are *good* give head? Can a woman be *good* at giving head, but still be *bad* in bed?

Finally, I interviewed the oldest professionals, because even in the sexy "yes" years of the 1970's, men still go to hookers and call girls for sex, and I wondered what dollars buy in bed. So I interviewed a brothel madam about her methods of selecting and training her girls to be *good*. A twenty-three-year-old hooker on her secret techniques and the sex acts she refuses. A pimp on why he thinks whores are better in bed, what skills make a whore *good* and the one practice a whore is forbidden to refuse. A Hollywood hooker on her special clients and her methods of helping men act out their fantasies. A Las Vegas hooker on her most sensational ways of pleasing a man, her advice for other women who want to be good in bed, and what men must do to make *her* come. A Beverly Hills call girl on how she enacts men's most bizarre sexual fantasies, and the one inhibition she still retains herself.

A male hooker on why women pay to go to bed with him, their fears about being *good,* the ways a man can tell, without touching a woman, if she is going to be *good* in bed, and his advice for every woman who is scared of not being sexually perfect.

The process of writing this book was filled with excitement and drama for me; there were many high points, like Robert Mitchum at the Hollywood Golden Globe Awards ("I'm glad you asked"); like talking to other women and discovering that their insecurities matched mine; high points like an interview with Vidal Sassoon at his house in Beverly Hills, with advice about hair thrown in; like learning sexual secrets from hookers in a Nevada brothel, seeing them line up for the men, and feeling kinky because *I* was the only woman who was dressed.

There were high points like meeting my teenage idol, Richard Burton, backstage at a Broadway theater; talking to Jack Nicholson at a party for Harry Reems; Marilyn Chambers and Fanne Foxe both unafraid to admit their insecurities, but still able to pass on techniques and advice; high points like Engelbert Humperdinck picking me out of an audience of eleven hundred people at the Riviera Hotel in Las Vegas, singing to me onstage, kissing me, and inviting me backstage, giving me the ideal opportunity to ask him my question.

The low points were never very low, because I was so caught up in the excitement of the project. But there still were some down moments; moments like trying to interview Burt Reynolds, driving four hundred miles, narrowly escaping rape, deportation, and arrest, and still failing to get anywhere near Burt; moments like a confrontation with a highway patrolman who stopped me for speeding at five in the morning on the road to Las Vegas, answered my question, loved the book, but still gave me a ticket; like asking celebrities who avoided my question: Peter Falk ("What makes a woman G.I.B? The color of her tie."), Doris Day ("What makes a woman G.I.B? I don't want to get into that.") Helen Reddy ("What makes a woman G.I.B? No comment.") and Mary Tyler Moore, who started to give me a sincere answer, but was stopped by Ted Knight, who cut in and told her to answer "Crackers"—which she did.

There were low points in my day-to-day life: like moving out of my apartment, being invited to sleep on a friend's floor, which was lovely except that the floor was in a nudist camp, where I ended up in the middle of December with lots of grey-bearded middle-aged attorneys from Marina Del Rey wandering around, pretending not to look, then asking me if I was into multiple relationships.

My private life changed slightly because of the book, and with my discovery that there is no such thing as a formula fuck. There were sexual situations I walked away from—whereas before I would have stayed. There were sexual fantasies I acted out, whereas before I would have been afraid to. At times, the book itself seemed like a fantasy I was acting out.

But, more than anything else, the book has been an adventure for me. It has been full of adventure, full of reassurance, full of advice. Full of opinions from experts, full of hints from hookers. Full of insecurities from women I had never dreamed were insecure. Full of honesty from celebrities I had never dreamed were honest. Full of dreams and fantasy figures, stars and sex symbols, celebrities and glitter. Full of men I had fantasized about—and women I had fantasized being. Full of men I wanted—and women I wanted to be. Full of change, full of contrast, full of glamor, full of reality. My adventure. And yours.

Part I

The Medical Professionals

GYNECOLOGIST

This interview is with a gynecologist. For professional reasons, I can't reveal his name.

The woman who is good in bed is not recognizable when I examine her. There is no such thing as a superior cunt, even though men do fantasize about a woman's cunt being cute and neat, with symmetrical hair. Ultimately, the only thing relevant is that the clitoris responds; I have never seen one that didn't, and I have even seen patients whose clitorises have been amputated who were still able to have orgasms.

But some women feel that the vagina is a kind of cesspool; they insist on douching once a day, and ignore the fact that they have vaginas at all. I see women all the time who are uncomfortable with the idea of examining themselves, know nothing about what goes on below their bellybutton, and are even ignorant about where the vagina ends. I've seen women who have panicked because they have lost the string of their tampon and believe it is going to disappear forever.

Women see their sex organs as an absence rather than a presence. Men are proud of their penises. They have a totally different attitude because a penis is an obvious separate entity.

The vagina is an ingrowth, not an outgrowth, and for some women it has the same connotations as the rectum: moist, internal, even dirty. This affects their attitudes toward their own sexuality.

In their childhood, women develop inhibitions that prevent them from being good. If a mother sees her son playing with himself, she says "No," but means "Yes," with an undertone of "Isn't he cute, he's finally found himself." But if a mother catches her daughter fondling her clitoris, she is far less permissive and forbids her to touch that "nasty, dirty crack down there." Thus is born the whole attitude in a woman that touching and exploring herself is taboo, that a man's penis is great, but a woman's clitoris is dirty. I've been with women who have said, "Don't give me head, I haven't had a bath." Women have to eradicate those inhibitions before they can be sexually free.

Women also worry, at times, what their vaginas taste like when a man goes down on them. I don't think there is any kind of composition that scientifically contributes to taste. I don't think some vaginas taste better than others, but they do taste different because some women have vaginal discharges, which obviously affect the smell or taste of the vagina. A healthy vagina tastes kind of neutral, like mucous membrane tastes anywhere, like the inside of a mouth.

I don't get clues about a woman's responsiveness when I examine her. I am in a lot of trouble if I do. Women come into my office and say, "I hate these examinations." I say, "If you liked it, you'd have to leave." It is generally not a sexual experience to be examined.

I was able to tell about a woman sexually just once. This woman was very apprehensive about whether she and her husband would be able to stay together sexually—she felt that she was losing her prowess. She used to do the vaginal Kegel exercises, and when I put my finger in her vagina to examine her, it was totally imprisoned. I thought she was going to break it, she was that powerful. I could only assume that she would be dynamite as far as holding onto a man's prick in bed, except that it was all very much contrived, and it seemed as though she was trying to be what she *thought* was terrific in bed.

But all the technique in the world is valueless unless the woman is turned on. Lubrication is the woman's equivalent to a male erection, and if she is not lubricated she is not genuinely turned on, no matter what her head tells her. Every woman, in general, has the same basic capacity for lubrication, which is always regulated by the degree of sexual turn-on.

Everything is variable according to the way a woman feels about the experience she is having; even the orgasmic speed of a woman masturbating with a vibrator depends on her feelings about vibrators. The length of time it takes for a woman to come will differ from one experience to another.

There is no such thing as a woman who takes a long time to come. There is no fixed time span, but a woman will obviously take less time with somebody she feels close to and is turned on by. There is no absolute, and the woman who goes into a situation and says, "It takes me a long time to come" is deceiving herself.

The orgasm is a very complex mechanism. It is very important not to cater to the guy who says, "Yes, I know it takes you a long time to come." He is not recognizing that maybe *he* is not doing it in a way to turn the woman on. Or perhaps the woman is deliberately delaying the orgasm so that the sex will last longer. Or maybe she is frightened of her own orgasms, because she knows she shouts and screams when she comes and she doesn't want to shout and scream in front of *that* particular man. Also, an orgasm is not always pleasurable for a woman. If the uterus contracts, it actually may be uncomfortable.

Every woman has a different orgasm from every other woman, and she will have a different kind of orgasm at different times. There are times when a woman will get very turned on and not have an orgasm and there are times when she is not so turned on, yet she will still have orgasms.

Other women are not orgasmic. That is the technical definition of frigid, but they may be frigid with one person and terribly turned on with somebody else.

Some men are desperate for a woman to have an orgasm; they are unfulfilled unless they have succeeded. To men like that, sex is just another goal-oriented commercial venture in which the woman's orgasm validates them: "I made it, I scored another point." Women realize this and they fake to allow the guy to believe he is a success, because they think the man won't come back to them if he realizes he has failed. So Academy Awards are really given to the wrong people. They should be presented to all those women who fake that they have had a wonderful time in bed.

Deception is often involved in sex. For some men, the holding, the stroking, and the caressing are a lot of learned behavior which they use as a means to an end, as a weapon to get to bed with a lady. Then, once they are in bed, much of the cuddling is done as a pat on the head. If a man is aroused, he has his orgasm, and he gets his satisfaction fairly quickly. Then he is ready to turn over and go to sleep, or to put his pants on and go home.

Some women take a package to bed every time and always do X, Y, and Z. When women like that go to bed, they give a man oral sex as a duty, not because they like it, but because it goes with X and Y. They don't do it because they are enthusiastic about oral sex, but because they just want to please, to give, to get.

The woman who is good in bed has pride in her own sexuality, her own sex organs, and is turned on by the man she is in bed with. Most women are good at least once—the first time you go to bed with them. That is because of the conquest, the expectation and the finding out, the learning, the new skin, the titillation. Every woman is good in bed the first time, and also if you haven't been with her in a long while. But in order for the man to want to go back and be continually aroused, the woman has to be more than good.

The feeling of connectiveness matters and the relationship itself. A woman's looks—her equipment—only matter in the arousal stage, not in the delivery, because everything dissolves when you are inside the lady. Then your perception of whether she has nice tits, ass, or legs dissolves into how you are feeling about the experience.

Because I've been in this business so long, part of the fantasy other men have about sex has been taken away from me. When you look at vaginas all day long, it is hard to fantasize about them. But my profession has made me ultimately more healthy. I am much more interested in the woman's personality and in my feelings for her. That's what makes her good, not her vagina.

SYLVIA KARS

Sex Surrogate

Sylvia Kars has been a sexual surrogate for three and a half years. Men with sexual dysfunctions are referred to her, and she acts as a partner to try and resolve them.

A sex surrogate has to be trained formally, and my experience has given me an insight into what makes a woman good. I also work with men whose sexual problems have been caused by the woman who is bad in bed. That kind of woman castrates. She makes fun of the penis being too small, or talks about other men being better in bed, or she demands things and comes on too strong with shy men.

Demands in bed can ruin a sexual relationship. Both partners should communicate their desires verbally, but neither partner should insist; I get angry if a man demands that I have more than one orgasm. I am convinced that the best relationships happen when neither partner forces his or her own value system on the other.

The woman who is good enjoys foreplay and doesn't always expect rockets to go off every time.

A great many women have difficulty in attaining orgasm during intercourse, and they become afraid that they are taking too long. A woman should communicate to her partner: "I am worried that it is taking me too long. Please tell me if you are bored or tired." Then, if the woman loses the time fixation in her mind, she will get an orgasm. When a woman expresses her anxiety to the man, that her orgasm requires too much time, she will lessen her feeling of responsibility and then she can relax. She should make a contract with the man that if *he* wants to stop, he should tell her beforehand so she won't feel rejected.

Fear of rejection often prevents women from experimenting in bed. Sometimes they are afraid of attaining satisfaction because they feel that there will be an obligation if they get what they want in bed. Many women have difficulty in surrendering to their partners, whether for an evening or for a lifetime. Those kinds of women feel that if they give in to their partners—let go in bed—the partners will be able to control them. This, essentially, is a fantasy which prevents them from being good in bed.

If a woman had never been to bed with a man and wanted to

be good, I would advise her to be her own best lover; to be in touch with her own body and to know what makes her feel good; to be an expert at masturbation.

The woman who wants to be good must enjoy whatever she and her partner do in bed and shouldn't demand anything over and above that; she must be willing to masturbate if the man doesn't satisfy her, or be satisfied by oral sex and not demand that a man's penis perform on all occasions for as much time as she *wants* to be fucked.

A woman who is good gives a man a lot of acceptance to do and be whatever he is at that particular moment.

DANNY TOMPKINS

Sex Surrogate

Danny Tompkins is one of the few male sexual surrogates practicing in America. He helps women overcome their sexual problems by reeducating them about their sexual attitudes. The women are referred to him by therapists, and intercourse rarely takes place between Danny and his patients.

Women have hang-ups about being good in bed. They are also often afraid that men will laugh at their bodies, but they should remember that sexual satisfaction is strongly related to good physical health. And that doesn't necessarily mean that a woman needs to look like a centerfold model to be good in bed.

Before undressing, I talk to thc client about sex, get her to reveal where she is at. She may have inhibitions which reflect themselves in sex and in a feeling that sex is dirty. I try to get the woman to feel good about herself and lose some of those inhibitions. When we undress, I play with the woman in a safe way, but we might go through six or eight hours (the course takes fifteen) before touching the erogenous zones.

None of the women who have come to me needed sex therapy—the problem was primarily insecurity and fear. They had emotional problems. They were hypertense, hyperactive, couldn't relax in bed, and I cured them by giving them relaxing exercises which are allied to self-hypnosis.

Many women who come to me have difficulty in having orgasms via intercourse. Actually, most women don't get orgasms through intercourse anyway, mostly only through manual manipulation or oral sex. Women should learn not to just concentrate on the goal, but also to appreciate the quality of the route: sensuality, foreplay, the sensitivity of one partner to another.

The time it takes to reach an orgasm varies from woman to woman. The time it takes is very tied up with the way a woman feels about the relationship, so she may not even be able to have an orgasm with some men with whom she has a bad relationship. It is important, though, not to stick to one particular preferred sexual position, because that can lead to hang-ups and then the woman will only attain orgasm in that one position. She should also vary her style in masturbation, and not always do it with the same hand.

If I had to educate a woman so that she wouldn't worry about being good, I would teach her that it is only natural for people to fuck, that there are other ways to play besides concentrating on the central theme, and that everything is all right as long as it feels good and satisfies you.

CAROL DOWNER

Feminist

Carol Downer runs the Los Angeles Feminist Woman's Health Center. Over the past five years, she has taught hundreds of women to examine their own vaginas with the use of a speculum and a mirror.

The stereotype of a woman who is good in bed is still a woman who reflects a man's desires. I believe that every woman has done something at one time in her life in order to be good in bed: letting a man touch her when she didn't want him to, having sex when she felt tired, not asking for what she wanted in bed. At the center we have been measuring our libidos, and some of us find that we rarely have sex at the times when our libidos are at their height, because the timing of sex is determined by the man's libido—when *he* wants to have sex.

Sometimes, just for fun, I will ask a self-examination group to raise their hands if they have *never* faked an orgasm. I have never yet seen a hand raised by any woman.

A lot of women fake because they are afraid to say that they didn't come, so they just give up and fake. Women fake all the time in bed, to be good for men. I don't think most women get orgasms with straight fucking anyway, mostly just manually or orally.

Women have to alter their attitudes to their genitals before they can really enjoy sex, to forget those years of not looking at their sex organs and being taught to keep their skirts over their knees while their male peers were comparing each other's penises. The whole attitude of women to their genitals is one of self-disgust. Women know more about a man's penis, are more willing to touch it, than they are willing to touch or look at their own sex organs. Learning to like a penis and dislike their own sex organs is a cultivated taste that women develop over a period of time, just as people learn to appreciate classical music.

It is very dramatic when we do self-examination. The women go from mild shock and distaste to intense curiosity. At first, some women have difficulty even in opening their legs, they are so conditioned to keeping them closed. Women *do* worry about being good in bed, but what they really mean by that is "pleasing the man." But before they can even do that they need to recover from years of self-disgust. Our conditioning still takes over; one of the women in the group lost total control the first time a man gave her oral sex, and she urinated. The man accepted it, but the self-disgust remains for her, and for the many other women who are ashamed of their own bodies and their sexuality.

STEVE ZAX
Plastic Surgeon

Steve Zax is a celebrated Beverly Hills plastic surgeon whose skill has tranformed the features and figures of many of Hollywood's top stars. He is in his thirties, attractive, and married to a very beautiful woman who is a former Miss Greece.

If I, as a plastic surgeon, could create the ideal woman in bed, she would be five-feet-six-inches tall, she would weigh 115 to 120 pounds, and she would have soft skin, open eyes—regardless of color—a bust that is ample but not exaggerated, smaller rather than larger hips, and a quick, smooth body. She would have an air of eagerness about her; the woman who is great in bed always has an eagerness of spirit about her. She is mostly able to enjoy sex with less mental or physical hang-ups.

If a man is lucky, he will meet one woman in his life who is great in bed. Usually she will also please him esthetically: her hair is like sunlight and Chablis wine, or her eyes are like the sea, or her body welcomes him and he cannot get enough of it, or her skin just keeps inviting him back and back.

A woman is great in bed if she has the ability to do whatever she may fantasize. We all have fantasies we carry around in our fantasy kits, our little black cases. A woman who is great lives out her fantasies and lets the man live out his. She has a wanton abandon, and will not refuse anything in bed. Refusal doesn't enter into her sexual relationships. Most men will get the chance to bed women who are good, but the woman who is great is something extraordinary.

The woman who is bad in bed just lays there; she doesn't respond, doesn't feel. Non-orgasmic women are often motivated by a feeling of "I dare you to show me; I dare you to make me; you can't do it"; they are throwing out a challenge to a man. They want to create a situation where the man really has to work to bring her to orgasm with every subtle nuance, with great energy and imagination. There is some excitement in the idea that "I am going to be the one who makes this woman have an orgasm. I am going to do it, because she says she can only do it once in two hours." Most men, initially, will find that a challenge (which it is meant to be). But, after a while, it gets physically exhausting.

Great sex is very much like what the Indian writer Tagore described in a book called *Fireflies:* "The butterfly that a man captures is one that eludes him his entire life; but the one that is free, that he can never grasp, is his forever." It is a matter of making the moment last, trying to drill some perpetuity into that moment, knowing all the time that it is temporary, that it is fleeting, that it may never come again. What matters in bed is a moment full of feeling, what we feel. What we hear doesn't have to be moans or screams or cries, but sometimes whispers—not only all the forbidden words. (If you read *The Story of O*, there is not one "dirty" word in it, yet it's a most erotic book.) The whispers appeal to one of the five senses, and the five senses really matter: the whole mental set, the perceptive set, what you can smell and taste and feel and think and see.

If we can see the woman we are making love to, and if we can see ourselves *with* that person, that is a tremendous source of stimulation, because some women will let you *see* how much they are excited. It's tremendously exciting to be with a woman who is good, to see her enjoying herself and enjoying you, watch all the colors change like all the colors of the rainbow, from the beginning to the final moment. It's beautiful. And the woman who is great in bed lets you see yourself in her eyes. When you are with a woman who is great in bed, the sex is all in your head. It's what is between your ears that matters, not what is between your thighs.

PAULINE ABRAMS

Sex Therapist

Pauline Abrams is a well-known sex therapist in New York City. She is a writer and a lecturer, and has done a considerable amount of research in psychosexual behavior.

I am thirty-eight. When I was growing up, a woman didn't have to be good in bed—she just had to be *married*. We were told that once we were married, we could go to bed; then, when we were finally *in* bed we were allowed to open our legs. But no one ever told us that we were expected to open them *well*. Today's generation are growing up with the idea that they have to be good. This creates tremendous pressures and performance anxieties every time they go to bed, ultimately making them just as tense as the older generation.

Women believe all sorts of garbage about what makes them good in bed: that they have to give a man an erection at the drop of a hat, that they themselves have to be instantly orgasmic. Women have been raised to feel that sex is not their due, so they will let men do anything that isn't painful, even though they may be uncomfortable or bored. Women also tend to think, "If I were really good in bed, he would never want to sleep with another woman"—and that being good means being the best.

The woman who really *is* good in bed is often recognizable because she is prepared to talk freely to her partner about her own personal sexual experiences.

There is no correlation between the size of a woman's clitoris and her sexual enjoyment or orgasmic capacity. In fact, there are very few absolutes governing the woman who is good in bed. I think she has to enjoy sex, because if she doesn't, her partner won't. She has to enjoy oral sex, and she has to be sensual, responsive, and abandoned, with the capacity for communication.

The woman who is good is abandoned. She is vocal, makes noises, and does not feel ashamed of any part of her body, or anything that is part of the sex act. She has to abandon herself to lust, and not many people can do that. Being good is not a technique—it is a way of responding, of feeling good about your partner and being sensitive to his needs. The woman who is good is responsive in bed, but being responsive does *not* necessarily mean being orgasmic. The orgasm is not a response to the man's excellent technique; it is the result of a multiplicity of factors.

Being orgasmic is not what makes a woman good in bed. There are some men who believe it does; but men like that don't really give a damn about the woman—it's their own ego that is invested in the woman's orgasms—and those men wear the woman's orgasms like medals on their chests. They place pressure on a woman to come, as in the old Lenny Bruce line: "Did you come? Did you come? Did you come, come come?"; in fact, the woman's orgasmic capacity is totally irrelevant to the question of whether or not she is good in bed.

Some women are just not very orgasmic, and some women feel less good if they fail to have an orgasm. Other women have a credit system where they feel the man owes them an orgasm; unless these women come, they feel that they didn't get their money's worth. That's absurd, because few men are responsible for the physiological capacity their partner has for orgasm.

I feel that a woman is responsible for her own orgasm. If she doesn't come, and it bothers her, she should masturbate. That will make some men insecure, but those men are insecure to begin with. I like to give my vibrator to my lover. But I have my best orgasms if I put a dildo inside me, so that it touches my cervix, and then use the vibrator. That makes my orgasms much stronger.

There is no fixed time span for each individual's orgasm. It always varies, but women are constantly bugged by thinking, "Is he bored?" "How do I know he is enjoying what he is doing?" "Maybe he really wants to stop?" I am just like any other woman and I feel the same way until I have built up a strong relationship of trust. Sometimes I don't come at all. When a woman worries ("Maybe his hand is tired?" "Maybe his mouth is tired?"), she stops her orgasm or slows it down.

The orgasmic time span is different with every woman at different times. It even alters in masturbation. Some days I come in thirty seconds; other days I know exactly what it's like to be an impotent male: I put my hand on my clitoris and I can't feel a thing. It takes longer for me to come with a vibrator, because I can't control the feedback system as well as with my own hand. The feedback system is also far less reliable when some other hand is on you; you get very, very close and if you were masturbating yourself you would know exactly what to do. You may have been close to an orgasm a hundred times, but the man keeps going off a fraction. It's annoying.

Women take longer to achieve orgasm during masturbation than men; but in intercourse the feedback system is much less accurate for women than it is for men because the slightest error in movement takes the hand away from the center of excitation, which is the clitoris.

Every woman has a different kind of orgasm. Some women are multi-orgasmic, and each orgasm becomes more and more powerful. So they keep wanting orgasms, because the next one is always better than the last. Women like that often have orgasms that appear very meaningless, and sometimes they don't even know that they have come.

I have an orgasm like a man: once I have had it, my libido is spent and I am not interested in sex for quite a while. So I would much rather continue to make love and not have my orgasm. I once had a marvelous lover who suddenly announced that he was going to make me multi-orgasmic. But, knowing that my orgasm was so vital for him (this wasn't conscious), I never came at all with him.

There are partners with whom I am 100 percent orgasmic—nothing gets in the way; my head never works, just my body. Trust matters, but it can work negatively. Some women have affectional response. They can't come with men they love and they are unable to abandon themselves because they feel that the man is judging them, whereas they can abandon themselves totally and come very easily with men they don't give a damn about.

I am not always orgasmic, especially if the trust has been destroyed. My second husband was very virile. I used to come as soon as he did, and he would still have an erection afterwards. Then we were divorced, but we still continued an affair. One day, in a moment of anger, he said: "Sex therapist, sex therapist, for *years* I have been faking." And then he told me that he had faked orgasm in order to get me to come. I don't know how true that was, but once he had told me, I never came with my ex-husband again, ever. Every time he came I would think, "Maybe he is faking," and so I became nonorgasmic with the same man with whom I had always been 100 percent orgasmic.

I've still got places to go sexually—I become increasingly more abandoned each year. Sexual growth is in a state of flux, it's very dynamic, and we never stop growing. Experimentation leads to sexual growth, and the woman who is good will always experiment. She will be open to fantasies, role playing, and dressing up (men really do like women in black garters and silk stockings). The woman who is good should accommodate her partner's sex fantasies and live out her own; she should try everything a few times (I don't know what a few times is, but I sure as hell know it means more than once or twice).

Men want to try anal sex; the woman who is good will give it a try until she can objectively make up her mind. I don't like swallowing male ejaculate, but if I am in a relationship for a lengthy period of time and it appears important to the man for me to swallow, I try. I have discovered that telling a man that swallowing his ejaculate makes me throw up generally makes him incapable of ejaculating in my mouth in the future. Men are as sensitive as women, and caring lovers do not want to put their partners through any unpleasant experiences. Usually, though, unless they have to come in the open air, men don't mind if I fail to swallow their ejaculate—it just has symbolic connotations. After a lengthy period of oral sex, most men are quite content to come in the woman's vagina.

A lesbian experience can teach a woman that her cunt is sensuous, not slimy and smelly. When a woman inserts her tongue or finger into another woman's cunt, she will find that it is really warm and moist and womblike. Her attitude alters. Ninety percent of all women hate their own genitals, and are ashamed of them. That's very common to women—I see surrogates who think that their cunts are ugly. But no man ever thinks his penis is ugly—he thinks it is the most important gift to women, that it rules the world. Women have a much more negative body image than men, especially in this glamor culture. I work in the nude most of the time, and I am very comfortable with my own body, but most women are not.

It is impossible to be good in bed if you have a bad body image. I teach a three-day workshop, and one of the courses is in sex consciousness-raising. People are surprisingly ashamed of their bodily functions: farting, having to go to the bathroom, using almost the same equipment with which they go to the bathroom for sex. They feel guilty and ashamed.

Through therapy and education I teach people to stop letting their heads bother them, to be freer. I teach techniques in communication. The woman who is good is able to communicate her sexual desires. I teach people to say the things that embarrass them. For example: "I would love to go down on you, but would you mind taking a shower first?" Or, "I'd love to kiss you, but would you mind brushing your teeth first?" People have incredible problems regarding sexual communication.

Women are also very ignorant about their own bodies. They are unfamiliar with their functions. For example, every woman who wants to be good should insert her finger into her vagina and taste her own vaginal mucosa for cleanliness. I don't think she should go to bed before she has tasted herself, just as she shouldn't go to bed before she has brushed her teeth. A woman should also become familiar with the man's sexual functions; she should remember that men differ sexually according to their age.

Boys of eighteen are tremendously anxious. They get erections easily, but they can lose them through nervousness. The older man maintains his erection, but he may not always ejaculate every time he has intercourse. The amount of ejaculate is lessened, as is its strength. Most importantly, the older man doesn't respond very cerebrally, and he requires more tactile stimulation. He doesn't get turned on by looking at a naked woman—he gets turned on when she touches him. It is unrealistic for a woman to lie down next to an older man and expect him to respond instantly with an erection.

The woman who is bad in bed has high, unrealistic expectations of a man. She is a castrating bitch and criticizes him constantly. We have patients whose girlfriends always sit in judgment of them. Then the man becomes terrified of every move he makes. The woman deballs him; she is bad because she is ignorant.

Embarrassment at her own body and her sexual feelings make a woman bad. She doesn't move, she hates her own body, and she doesn't make sounds. She doesn't communicate verbally, and she fails to respond. She has bad muscle tone in her vagina, and she is unable to grip the man with it. The woman who is good, however, thinks of her vagina as a sensuous tool which she uses to give a man pleasure; therefore she exercises to improve its muscle tone.

The ultimate virtue of the woman who is good in bed is that she has no fixed criteria for being good. The woman who is good doesn't take a set of rules to bed with her. She knows that every sexual experience is unique and that every time she goes to bed, even with the same person, the sex will be different. There are only two kinds of sex—good and bad—and good sex is always different.

Part II

The Celebrities

OLIVER REED

I felt a bit guilty when I met Oliver Reed because a friend of mine had just arranged for a pie to be thrown in his face. We met and then had a very bad dinner in Beverly Hills, which helped me get over my guilt. We realized that the dinner was going to be bad the moment we read the menu. Oliver and I both wanted to leave, but the maitre d' was so overwhelmed to have Oliver in his restaurant that Oliver couldn't bring himself to walk out. So, despite the mention of slaves and abuse in the following interview, that evening Oliver Reed was very careful not to hurt anyone's feelings.

A woman is good in bed if she accepts the fact that she is going to be fucked. She is the receiver, the vessel, and provided that a woman understands that *she* is going to be penetrated, that she will always be fucked, then a man can have a proper sexual relationship with her.

I am very Victorian in my habits. I have never ever in my life been interested in anything small—in intellect, ideology, sociology, politics, in motor cars, hotel bills, in drinking habits, and certainly not in my ladies. My ladies should be luscious. My ladies should be voluptuous. I like large arses. I prefer large vessels, but not empty vessels. The fashion for thin ladies is only recent. The Pre-Raphaelite, full-hipped ladies of Holman-Hunt were my kind of women. Those used to be the fashionable style of woman, not the wishy-washy, complacent, high-titted society ladies.

Complacency makes a woman bad in bed. I can't tell if a woman is good by just looking at her. But one of the first signs of a woman who might be good is that she has made an effort for the man, that before seeing him she brushes her hair, puts all that shiny stuff on her lips, wears a fresh frock, covers herself with scent, then rushes out to meet him, and pretends that she is a lady.

Age makes a woman good in bed. A boy of seventeen wants to go to bed with a woman of twenty-seven to feel that an older woman is teaching him to make love. A man in his thirties and forties needs the complacency of knowing he can cope with a forty-year-old woman, but at the same time still retains the arrogance of a man who loves to tell himself he has copulated with a woman of under twenty-five.

Romance matters: those mornings with toast and marmalade in bed, when the woman gets back into bed with you and reads the papers. And there are toast crumbs in the bed, and she is very warm, breathing on your shoulder. So you smile and you wake up twenty minutes before the pubs open and she puts on some Mulligatawny soup in the kitchen, and you fall into the bathroom naked and she falls out of the kitchen naked. Then she puts on a clean frock and you go and play darts in a pub that is full of smoke and you know that you have just left toast crumbs in your bed. That is romance. The romance of going out to an Indian meal, then the movies, and after that, making love for the rest of Sunday. I think *that* is romance that has to be perpetuated through Monday and Tuesday, and I am not literate enough to understand what happens beyond Wednesday.

I don't think a woman would ever refuse something I wanted in bed. But I think that a woman is possibly less good if she *asks* for what she wants in bed. A woman always wants to be dominated in bed, but is afraid to admit it. So she says: "I want more" and shuffles around the bed, because she has read lots of cheap literature which says that a man is going to ejaculate eight times during the evening if he is James Bond, and no fewer than four times if he is of lesser note. Whereas in reality it will probably, in general, happen once; he will then fall asleep, and later it will happen again twice. A woman should never ever be demanding in bed.

A woman has to understand that in a man's sexual head she is the one who is going to be dominated and abused. A woman *should* be abused, and the woman who is happily abused is a successful lady in bed. I think the woman who is good in bed has to be quite a good slave. She also has to be a willing slave. A willing slave is always warm and humble and submissive and happy to be a slave—and being *that* is what makes a woman good in bed.

DAVID NIVEN

What makes a woman G.I.B? To be on the same wavelength as the man she is in bed with, whatever that wavelength may be.

CHARLES AZNAVOUR

I had already met French superstar Charles Aznavour when he was rehearsing for a concert at the Festival Hall in London. We did this interview in Los Angeles. His teenage daughter was with him, and the interview was done in her presence.

Napoleon used to say: "There are no bad armies, only bad generals." One thing I can say, without being too pretentious, is that every woman I have had has been fantastic in bed. I don't believe there is such a thing as a frigid woman. The approach of the man makes a woman good. If she is at all hysterical, then she is not good—she has to be the right partner.

Young women, teenage, are best. I prefer them. I am not at all homosexual, but I like boyish women, unformed, not exactly finished. Every man has a Pygmalion ego, or a mother complex. For my Pygmalion ego, I like to have a teenager in bed. For me, a woman is good if she knows nothing, and is open to everything.

My approach to a woman is always Pygmalion-like: I want to build her and teach her everything about life, everything about love, and something about bed. Most of the time a man builds the woman he wants to have in bed.

Sex is American; in Europe we talk about love. I can't tell if a woman is going to be good in advance. Sometimes I meet a woman and I think she is going to be fantastic, but that is all looks and not reality. Basically I think that the rapport is as important as bed is. Bed can't be the first condition for a man's love. Love is not as instant as some people believe. We meet someone, then we say to ourselves, without knowing it: "I have to be with her." Then we build. It is a projection.

The trouble is, though, that sexual failures begin with the

father, because we never talk about sex to our daughters, and most fathers protect their daughters' virtue. I think that is wrong, as it creates a guilt complex in a daughter's mind. How can a man who loves his daughter give her a guilt complex about sex? In the end I believe what makes a woman good in bed is happiness, being relaxed, and the ability to bloom like a flower.

JOHN WAYNE

What makes a woman G.I.B.? Being there.

FANNE FOXE

Fanne Foxe and I had tea at the Plaza, and before we started talking about what makes a woman good, we discussed the lure of the older man in great detail, although we were extremely careful not to specify which *particular older man we were talking about. Fanne was very bright and bubbly. She had an innocence about her that her P.R. man had mentioned, but that I was surprised to find actually did exist.*

I am not frigid, but men have sometimes made me feel insecure. I am an old-fashioned girl in bed, and it takes me a long time to warm up. I need romance, kissing, dancing, talking, and holding hands. I came from a very conservative family, and I was never taught what sex was all about, apart from the medical terms. I thought making love was just kissing. I never knew how to relax. I didn't even know how to reach satisfaction.

A lot of people thought that because I was a stripper, I would know all the tricks, that dancers are better in bed—like being a geisha, educated to please a man. But a woman doesn't learn to be good in bed working as a stripper. There is no way to learn. But if a woman is married for ten years to the same man, there's no chance of ever improving her sexual life. It goes down and down and becomes old-fashioned: the man on top of the woman, and that's it. Two and two are four, and "I'll see you tomorrow." I was married to the same man for nineteen years.

I think I enjoy sex much better now for what sex is. I think I have become better in bed for myself. I think for the man I am just about the same—neither worse nor better. I used to need to be in love before I had sex; now I am different and don't need to be. But with my old friend, it was not sex. We did make it, but it was not sex involved, it was something completely different: love, and the need for companionship. I satisfied him because he satisfied me. It was a completely different feeling. When I was with him I was not the animal that we all have inside.

I believe an older man doesn't need a woman who is good in bed, they don't really care for that as much as a younger man. I think older men get shocked if a woman is too uninhibited. They just don't care for an uninhibited woman. That is why I am shy and reserved most of the time, though I am not inhibited at all, and I am not square. I just think that the older man is just as insecure as the woman is, and if the woman comes on too strong, it just turns him off sexually. If a woman goes to bed with a man, and is just too much of an animal, too much of a sexy woman, and goes "boom, boom, boom," then does it and is crazy, the man will say, "She does it all herself. I didn't do it. I made her happy, but I think everybody else would. It's her nature."

It doesn't worry me that it takes a long time for me to have an orgasm, because it seems to please my guys. But I never got used to oral sex being done to me, and I don't care for it. With my husband I was embarrassed. I gave him oral sex and he enjoyed it very much, but whenever he wanted to do it to me I just never cared for it. If a man wants a lot of oral sex, I still don't give him all he wants. But the man does like to know that whatever you do to him, you do it all the way. Though you may not care for it constantly, you can at least show that you are willing to please him once.

Not all men like oral sex. Some men don't, like my old friend. That relationship was straight from the beginning. He didn't care for me to do it to him, nor him to do it for me. I think a couple of times I did it for him, and he was pleased, but not overwhelmed. He did it a couple of times to me because he thought I wanted it. We didn't need that. If it was there, fine. If it wasn't, we didn't care. We had other things to do that were better than that for us. I just didn't do it. He never did, and we got to this understanding, so it was all right.

About 75 percent of the men I have been with like oral sex a lot. Maybe 50 percent of the men I have been with like to do it to me. Out of that, 25 percent almost demand to do it a little—at least kisses—the other 25 percent will be satisfied anyway. They will be frustrated if I don't let them do it, but they will accept that. Perhaps it has something to do with my body. Our organs are very tender and very sensitive, and I think it is one of our most sensitive organs. When I have had that touched, I feel pain even to my toes, my nerves. It's not really pleasant when it hurts. But when I have regular intercourse and I enjoy myself, it goes into my knees. It's lovely, nothing hurts. It's like you discharge everything you have. It's fantastic.

There is an old Argentinian saying which I believe in: "The

man who is satisfied at the table and in bed will always stay with a woman.'' When I want to keep a man, I just take him to bed. A woman who is good in bed should be intelligent enough to lead a man to do what she wants without being obvious. A woman should neither refuse or say yes to everything in bed. If you see the man going toward something that you don't want, change the subject to something that would be of more interest to him. That's the way I've been doing it, and I'll tell you I have been quite successful.

I have found very few men like to talk when they make love, and women do. Men get distracted easier than a woman does; their organs have all the sensitivity. Don't tell a man he's fantastic. Tell him you are pleased and that you like it: ''Oh, I like it, I like it,'' and if he hits something that you enjoy: ''Oh, yes, that's it.'' Let him know with just a few words where he is right and where he is wrong. A woman has to make a man feel that he is going to give her something special and she is going to enjoy it. Then he will feel more secure. Make a man feel like he is a man. But not at all times; sometimes make him feel like he is a little boy.

I have made many mistakes, though; sometimes I am independent for too long, and the men don't like that. And a little bit of the time they just drift away. But I correct mistakes by calling and apologizing, by being very feminine and nice. Men like a feminine woman—they want a woman to be sexy, but not in a way everyone will notice. Instead of wearing a short see-through dress, women should be elegant and show just a little something. They prefer a woman who shows she has the potential to be a madonna *and* a whore.

If a woman asked for my advice on how to be good in bed, I would tell her to change a lot, sexually. There are tremendous variations in the ways of making love, and it's up to the woman. If she is always the same, she becomes a little boring, no matter how good she is. If you see a fantastic show a thousand times, it will be no good any more. But if you go to see the show one day and a performer is different, then it becomes good—there's something extra for the imagination.

A woman should never be the same person. I believe that by not being the same woman, in the same mood, I can provide my mate with a little variation. I have been managing all my men like that. For example, there are times a woman has to be feminine and little, but not always, because a man does not like a woman that is little. I try to please a man, but if you change completely into a puppet, men don't like that. They want you to keep your individuality, but only to use it at certain times, not always. A man likes a woman who has temperament and character, but not all the time. It's up to the girl. That's part of growing up, to know which part to use at which time.

I always feel best with older men. I feel proud to be with them, they make me feel much younger, and I always say, "If this man has been alive for ten years longer than I have, he must know a lot more about life than I do." I need to have an older man for love. I think younger men are a little bit more superficial than older men. I always think a younger man looks for something I can't provide. It's very difficult for me to carry on a conversation with a younger man, and try and be interesting and pretty and practical at one time. Once I start talking about profound thoughts, from my heart and from my mind, younger men get bored. They listen to you for a little while, and then they try to get down to action. Not necessarily going to bed straight away, but they want to warm the kettle immediately. Older men are much more subtle. They work from the inside out—while younger men work from the outside in.

I think power attracts women. I am not very aggressive, so the man is never in my power. If, somehow, he ever is, then I don't care for him anymore. I don't like puppets. So the power of an older man attracts me. I like a challenge. I don't care for a person who is a garbage collector to say that I am pretty and intelligent, because his appreciation would not be of any value to me. Unless I get to know a person really well, and know that he is an intellectual, he is smart and intelligent, has the power to be president, but that circumstances put him into garbage collection instead of being president, I am not interested. Although you don't know how good or bad the president is, you certainly know that he must have some rare qualities to become president. I think I would have been attracted by Kennedy, not because he was president, but because he radiated that charm. I think he was not a genius; in my opinion my old friend is a genius, and that attracts me a lot.

I think I am intelligent and I am warm of heart, and when I find somebody who, like my old friend, finds it, oh, it puts me right up there in the sky. I say, "This man could have been president of the United States, and he thinks that *I* am intelligent.

PETER FINCH

What makes a woman G.I.B? Generosity makes both a man and a woman good. Selfishness never makes good sex.

VIDAL SASSOON

Internationally renowned hair tycoon and TV personality, Vidal Sassoon is the co-author with his beautiful and talented wife, Beverly, of the best-selling book A Year of Beauty and

Health. *I first met Beverly and Vidal when I came out to California, where they have their own TV talk show. The show's motto is "Look better, think better, and feel better with the Sassoons," and they have always been their own best advertisement. At the Sassoon house in Beverly Hills, the entire family live on a strict regime of salad and health foods, although one day Vidal's mother and I sneaked off to a movie and gorged ourselves on popcorn. During the time that I have known Beverly and Vidal, I have never seen them eat anything remotely fattening, nor have I ever seen Vidal cut hair (although Beverly did design a hairstyle especially for me).*

Sex is perspiration and animation. I think that, above all, sex is an art form. We should have legalized sex houses. People should be able to go to good sex houses and learn about sex in the same way as they are able to go to good restaurants and learn about food. Because the more you know about sex, the more exciting it becomes.

It is terribly important to help people over their sexual hang-ups and allow them to enjoy sex at the earliest age possible. When my son is fifteen, I would like to hand him over to a superb courtesan to learn all about sex. I know he will find out eventually. I first had sex at seventeen. I was a late starter, but I still didn't find out what it was all about until my late twenties. Prostitutes were out of the question because everyone kidded that you would get some vile disease. Anyway, I was too proud to pay for sex. I don't want my son to go through all sorts of sexual nonsense, first, because although experimenting can be a lot of fun, a young man needs to develop a lot of expertise to increase his own confidence.

I also don't want my daughter to get screwed up. Screwed is okay, so, if she asked my advice at sixteen or seventeen, although I couldn't be her pimp I would hope to find a gentle and experienced man to take her into hand. A girl can really be tortured as a virgin, if her first sexual experience goes badly.

One of the worst things about sex is getting used to doing it with a woman in a set specific manner. But the woman who is good can really turn a man on to nuances and stir up his imagination and feelings, either with gentleness, words, physical things, or mood. She creates an excitement. A woman who is good in bed can "get" to most men in the end. I used to work for Raymonde, the hairdresser, and he once said to me: "If you are having caviar every night, occasionally it is very good to have fish and chips." I think if a woman treats sex as an art form and is very explicit and innovative in the art of making love, then a man will stop looking for fish and chips and stick to caviar.

I truly think that over a long period of time, fit women are better in bed (a woman can have thick bones, yet have a muscular body with stamina). Over a long haul—a marvelous four-hour bash—the woman has to be fit, or else she is going to doze off exhausted after twenty minutes. There is a tremendous amount of physical exhaustion in sex at its best—not necessarily in acrobatics—but in the physical exertion and strength needed for good sex. Fit people are better at sex as long as they have everything else going for them, like desire and the urge, the appetite and the libido.

The thought of having sex with an older woman who has kept herself beautifully has always intrigued me. Ten years ago I saw Marlene Dietrich at Dior in Paris, and there was this most exotic woman. My fantasies run in that direction. Sex is a vibrant, youthful thing, done by people of all ages if they have kept themselves looking youthful and marvelous no matter what age they are. A sixty-year-old woman is good if she is experienced, but all a teenager needs are her youth and the charm of naivete, which turn a man on in bed.

I think hot-blooded women who make demands can be very exciting. If a woman refuses what I want in bed, then it is marvelous to be able to gently coerce her. It is a challenge, and I believe people need challenges in bed, except in new love, when everything is hot and the only thing one needs then is the moment in time. But in most sexual relationships, the more you have sex the more profound you become.

If a man is feeling strong, and everything is going along nicely, and he is in full control (because it is sometimes nice to be in complete control) he won't mind the woman taking a long time to come. But there is something marvelous about a woman having half a dozen orgasms to the man's one. That gives him a tremendous sense of being superman, even if it is just for that evening. If a girl doesn't come the first time we go to bed, then it is a challenge, something to make work the second time. Rather like with the girl who doesn't open her legs the first time you go out with her—the whole thing becomes a challenge.

A woman has to be happy at making love. You can never force that happiness. Some women are slightly animalistic at making love, and for them sex is one of the greatest experiences of all time. Very few women are frigid with everyone; therefore, if a woman is bad in bed with you, it may be because you are not turning her on, perhaps because the skin textures and the smells are incompatible.

If I were Frankenstein and able to create the ideal woman in bed, she would have Suzy Parker's legs and my wife Beverly's face. She would use her head in bed; sex is cerebral. If she had children and wasn't as tight as a virgin, she would use her legs and the muscles in her stomach and her back. Being good in bed is knowing what to do with what you have got.

I believe nothing is wrong in bed—nothing is bad. If you fail, you should just have a good laugh, because I think sex can be funny. Everybody, whoever they are, must have fouled up in bed once or twice. The grass is never really greener, because everyone has their problems, their off-days, and their marvelous days. No one is King Kong; there aren't any supermen or superwomen, so everyone should just view sex as something to look forward to: a super-plus.

ENGELBERT HUMPERDINCK

What makes a woman G.I.B? It isn't physical. It's in the eyes of the beholder—in the eyes of the woman. But what makes a woman good in bed also stems from the well-known American saying, "God grant me the serenity to accept the things I cannot change—the courage to change the things I can—and the wisdom to know the difference."

BEVERLY SASSOON

I learned about sex through experience. I was sixteen, and my first boyfriend was very good and made the whole experience pleasant. Unfortunately, so many of us were raised with the approach that sex is taboo; but getting over that and attaining mental freedom makes a woman good.

I don't know if I project being good in bed. You can be that without appearing flashy and showing a lot of cleavage. When I look at a man I feel I can tell if he would be good for me—but I don't know if he can do the same about me.

I really believe sex is just for two people. Group sex or orgies are not my scene. No one has ever asked me to take part in anything like that, and I think I make it very obvious by my attitude that *that* is not where I am at. If I were asked, I would say "No" or "Thank you" or "Goodbye." I have never ever been forced to do anything I didn't want in bed. I believe sex should be exciting and thrilling, but I don't need added attractions to improve it. I would never put myself into a situation with someone I didn't trust, or who didn't know what he was doing, and I would never let anyone intimidate me in bed in any way. For example, if someone was a celebrity or a big movie star, I would never let that intimidate me. There are a lot of people walking around the streets who are probably just as good, if not better, than a celebrity.

I don't think you need to *ask* for what you want in bed. I think if a woman has any sort of intelligence, she can lead a man into doing what she wants. I am not a big talker; I don't think it is necessary to talk a man into being excited; I think that can all be done without words. If a man is inexperienced, it is fairly easy to guide him.

The woman who is good makes the man feel sex is his whole responsibility, but doesn't necessarily leave it all totally up to him. He can *think* that he is taking all the initiative and doing wonderful, marvelous things on his own, whereas actually a lot of the initiative comes from the woman. That sounds a little deceitful, but it sometimes is necessary; although sex is not a game it has to be handled intelligently. I always need a fairly solid foundation with a man before we have sex, because I don't believe in jumping in and out of bed with different people.

I don't feel less good if I take a long time to come. The more time you can spend in bed, if you are enjoying sex, the better. Worrying sometimes prevents an orgasm, because you must relax and enjoy the moment. Then, if an orgasm still doesn't happen, it doesn't happen. There are times when people do ask you if you have come, which is a fair enough question, if they don't know. The best way to answer is to be honest, unless, of course, you feel the answer will completely crush the man.

There are times when I find that I am not physically interested in sex. My sexual desire is lessened when I feel that I am slightly overweight or when I see something about my body that I don't like. When I am really thin I feel terrific in bed. I am not saying that thin women are better in bed; it is just that I feel *I* am better when I am thin because when I am in good shape, I feel attractive for myself. Then it follows that I feel attractive for the man. I also think it is very important to know one's own body just as well as one knows the man's body.

If I had to give another woman general advice on how to be good in bed, I would say that sex is like riding a horse. You must let the man have his head.

MICHAEL CAINE

What makes a woman G.I.B? It has nothing to do with beauty. There is no way you can tell by looking at her.

LILY TOMLIN

Super-comedienne Lily Tomlin was nominated for an Academy Award for her role in Nashville. *I met her at the Golden Globe Awards in Hollywood where she gave me this interview and then again at the Grammys where she reread it and giggled a lot.*

What in my opinion makes a woman good? What makes a midget good? Let's talk about life, don't let's talk about sexist questions. Let's talk about what makes an amoeba good in bed. The main trouble is that women have to get the approval of the ruling class, which is the white male.

Men always expect you to suck them, but they don't suck. Anyway, I hate the phrase "She sucks." Most of us have or do. Newborn babies do, and most of us in our lives, including John Updike, have sought through the decades to find someone who would or does suck. The question of sucking is important, even if it is armpits and toes. Very few people will suck toes—they think it is foot fetishism. People don't want to suck toes and they don't want to talk about life.

ROSE MARIE

What makes a woman G.I.B? I would say the right man who loves her.

JIMMY CONNORS

Marjorie Wallace introduced me to Jimmy Connors while he was practicing for the Alan King Tournament at Ceasar's Palace in Las Vegas, and we talked between sets.

I am pretty picky about ladies. Part of my pickiness is that I like them not too skinny nor too fat—I like a little bit to hold on to. My own pickiness is that I know what I like, but I can't tell if a woman is good by just looking at her—only whether I want to get her into bed. Looks can be very deceiving.

I don't like a woman who is loud, and I don't think I have ever had a loud woman. I like sex very easy: no set times, no set anything. Timing is a very important word to me in bed. Sex is no good if one person likes it and the other person doesn't. I don't want a lady who hits me with the headache ploy: "I've got a headache; I can't tonight." There are some things you can get in the mood for *all* the time, and sex is one of them, if it's with the right person. I think feelings are very important. You don't have to be in love with a woman, but feeling and enjoyment come into it very much, even if it's just a one-night stand. Whatever the circumstances, I don't think the woman would be there unless she wanted to be, or unless she felt something in one way or another.

Faking is no good in bed. You do know if a woman is faking in bed, I guess, by performance, because you know what the feeling should be like on both parts. I guess a woman can say she's had an orgasm, but she really hasn't, and I would hate to be faked in that respect. I really would. That would be poor performance on my part, wouldn't it? What am I there for? Am I there just for my own satisfaction, or for both? Sex has to work both ways, and I have to be with someone I really like.

I don't know if female athletes are better in bed. Athletics and sports build one up and make one very firm. I don't know if I want to say flexible, but I am not saying athletes aren't flexible, and a lot of them are good in bed. I hate to get into chauvinism, but I don't think ladies are as strong as men, so athletics are tough on them mentally and physically. It's difficult for an athlete to have soft and smooth skin; it's tough on my skin. When you're out in the sun, it's tough on men, let alone ladies. For myself, I like ladies with very smooth, very soft skin I can nestle up to and cuddle with.

If I could choose the best woman in bed for me, I would like one lady: very soft, very smooth, very gentle, very cuddly, pinchable, squeezable, one that is very relaxed and very easy-going. Easy to be with —no pressure, either in bed or out. One that makes things easy for me—is equal, so that I am for her and she is for me. Above all, she must be a lady. I like ladies. I have always grown up to respect women, and you just treat them much different than you do men, in your attitude, in your tone of voice. Women, I guess, though, are a lot of people's downfall, and I am not going to say they are not mine. But I think behind every man there is a lady, and in my case it's off-court, and I need somebody there who is easy for me to be with, and easy for me to talk to, and doesn't just break my balls.

HUGH O'BRIAN

What makes a woman G.I.B? The same thing that makes her good in the kitchen: having the right man to cook for, and making sure that everything is properly prepared before it goes into the oven, and that it comes out on time.

SALLY KIRKLAND

Sally Kirkland is an ex-debutante and actress. She played Robert Redford's stripper girlfriend in The Sting; *she played a hooker in* Cinderella Liberty *with James Caan; she played Barbra Streisand's Communist girlfriend in* The Way We Were *and also appeared in* Bite the Bullet.

I don't know if I should still count, but I think I have been to bed with at least two hundred men. Sex is an art form. After two hundred men you have a built-in education in being good because every guy has taught you something. But you can never learn enough about sex, emotionally and physically. I started off as a dancer and could have been another Gypsy Rose Lee. In a way, I dance in bed, with rhythm. I know I could be a fantastic hooker if I didn't have society to consider. I would have wanted to be one of the great courtesans. I am very physical—I am a Scorpio, and Scorpios are sensualists.

I am really spiritual as well. I can just sit and look at a man without even touching him, and still get turned on. If you are turned on that way, sometimes you don't need the actual sex.

When I am interested in a man I go through long periods of just staring at him. If he says, "Don't do that," I give him up because then I know he can't cope with my curiosity and the mental exchange that matter so much. My mind is very important, and all I need from the man is enough love and imagination to get me going.

I am totally honest in bed. I know that has scared a lot of men away. I am an animal when it comes to sex; I tend to exhaust men with my insatiable desire. I had a relationship recently and was really in love with the guy, but one day he turned around and said: "I don't think I can satisfy you. You have more sexual energy than anyone I have ever met." And left.

I am never scared to ask for what I want in bed. I lay it on the line at the beginning and say: "This is what I like; now you tell me what you like." If they relax they will eventually tell me. I have only met a couple of men who really were as animal as I am, just into anything that is sensual, the farthest reaches of the imagination. I wouldn't put anything past me in bed, except perhaps animals.

I let the man know that I am experienced, so then he is aware that if he has hang-ups he doesn't have to have hang-ups with me. I am not your average middle-class virgin, so men know that they can act out all their fantasies with me. When my lovers happen, they are intense, but they are very few and far between. I stay away from married men, or men who want to be with me because they have heard that I am good.

I happen to love vibrators, but sometimes when I take one out in front of a man, I never see the guy again. I guess that may be because men might feel threatened. It really bores me when guys put sex into terminology. They ask if it is over, which is silly, because in some cases it goes on and on, and if you weren't getting places, you would have stopped and said: "Let's do something else."

I know I take a long time to come and I don't think that makes me less good. When men say, "Did you come?" I say to them, "You mustn't let it bother you; don't get hung up about it. It is very possible that I have, and will ten times more in the next hour." Men asking make me feel like one of Pavlov's dogs, to have to perform on cue. I suppose a lot of guys do equate "good" with the woman coming quickly. But I wonder if men really know what happens in that department, and whether they don't realize that some things are peaks and not orgasms. I go the opposite way the minute a guy focuses on how quick I am to come. I believe that lots of psychiatrists are working with women all over the world because somewhere along the line they have been made to feel sexually inadequate.

ROGER MOORE

What makes a woman G.I.B? A woman is good if she doesn't argue.

WILT CHAMBERLAIN

Wilt Chamberlain, basketball superstar and sports tycoon, lay on the floor as we talked and was very careful not to intimidate me with his height.

I can tell if I *want* to go to bed with a woman or not by looking at her, but it's very hard to tell if she will be good in bed until I get her there. I used to own nightclubs where many women were very exhibitionistic when they danced and would really move their bodies in a way relative to sexual suggestion. When I watched them I would say, "Wow, she must be terrific in bed." Not true at all. Since then, my experience has been that the woman who just sits home, knits, and is afraid to exhibit herself outside can be a lot better behind closed doors, on a one-to-one basis, because she has really dreamed and conceived of the different things she wants to do in bed. When she is free enough to have sex with someone, she is going to be much better than the girl who is up there on the dance floor shaking her body around, because *that* is partially her thrill and she is never very good in bed unless she has an audience.

For me, the time of day, the day itself, how I feel, and circumstances themselves can determine whether I want a girl in bed. Some women appeal to me at various times in my life, whereas at other times they just don't. There are, of course, attributes that are outstanding for every man, depending on what you like best. I myself like a good strong body; I like a woman who is symmetrical, not overly endowed in any one area, unless I have a certain craving at a particular time for that area. She can be any height, four feet to six feet, as long as she is in proportion.

Beauty enhances my enjoyment. A beautiful woman is much easier for me to be attracted to. I really prefer dark-haired girls with dark eyes, olive skin, nice legs, and nice strong buttocks which have a little protrusion. The breasts can be any size so long as they are firm and not altogether sagging. A sensuous, voluptuous mouth is definitely a turn-on.

My ideal girl in bed would be a young lady who is smart—well above average—independent, but extremely flexible. A pretty girl walking down the street does not attract me as much as a girl who has achieved something. Maybe because I have achieved things, achievement is important to me. I almost look for my counterpart in that particular way. Her achievement does not have to be totally professional, though. A girl who washes floors, if that is the best she can do, can turn me on.

I usually prefer a woman who is not so experienced because, as I think I am a little different from the average man, I like to have a chance to be more of a teacher to a young lady, and she is usually more susceptible to teaching if she doesn't know anything herself. A man likes the innocence and virtue of the untouched flower, who can't know what she is doing, believing that he is going to be the full master, so whatever she learns will be his responsibility. That is a great ego trip which I think all men go through from time to time.

Orgasm matters in bed. When I was younger it would worry me if a woman didn't come. I would feel inadequate as a lover, and that I really wasn't doing what was necessary. I always felt rather strongly about myself in that area, so I used to think: "Hey, if I can't make her have an orgasm, then there is something wrong with *her* and not with me.'' But I would still worry. Now I recognize the fact that some women are not blessed with having the same repetition in orgasms as others. Some women have very strong ones; other women don't have any at all, because they are never relaxed enough, or familiar enough with their own bodies to know what turns them on. I try to explain to those women that maybe they should get into masturbation. But I don't alter my opinion of a woman if she doesn't have an orgasm.

I think a woman has the right, as I do, to refuse anything in bed, but I *demand* a good reason why she has refused. She can't just say, ''I don't want to do that.'' I also think that through society and all the social bullshit, women are afraid to be a little bit demanding in their sexual trips. Although they are coming out a little bit today, and God bless them for that. But a lot of women have sex with men they don't really like or have real relationships with because they want to do sexual things they have never done with their lovers. They are afraid that if they ask their boyfriends or husbands they may be turned off and reject them. So women who feel that way do what they want sexually with a virtual stranger they don't care about.

I play a game with women and ask them if they are good in bed. Very few women really know and most will admit that, especially if a woman has not had many experiences to compare. If she says she doesn't know, then she is being honest. One of the answers women give when I ask them if they are good is: ''I guess so, I have never had any complaints.'' Which is a very stupid answer because most men never really complain to a woman they make love to. So, ''I have never had any complaints'' is a cop-out, because who the hell is going to complain? Anyway, ''good'' doesn't matter much to some men who still say: "There is never a bad piece, some are just better than others."

BOB NEWHART

What makes a woman G.I.B? You are probably asking one of the least experienced men in the world. I would suspect love makes a woman good.

JACK NICHOLSON

I met Oscar-winning actor Jack Nicholson at a Beverly Hills party in aid of porno star Harry Reems. Jack was surrounded by photographers and autograph hunters, so I was impressed by the intensity of his answer.

I think feeling makes a woman good in bed. If it's not real, don't do it. I have background in Reichian therapy, and that's pretty much what it boils down to. If you really don't feel something, don't fake it. Just stop right there, even if it's with your wife, because forced sex is liked forced energy of any kind: it doesn't really work. I think that sexuality and sexual expression are really units of energy that are communicable, just like you change the way you feel when somebody just looks at you. I think that the change is a real thing.

BURT LANCASTER

What makes a woman G.I.B? What I am thinking is too dirty.

ELKE SOMMER

Beautiful German film star Elke Sommer lives in Beverly Hills with her husband, author Joe Hyams.

Chemistry makes a woman good. If your knees shake when you see a guy, that's chemistry. After eleven years of marriage, instead of the knees shaking with a sense of novelty, you have a different feeling. It is not the heart fluttering any more. But you also don't need to perform any more either—you can relax and be yourself. You can be comfortable and not worry about your makeup and the way you look. If you are loved, then you have to be good in bed.

GLADYS KNIGHT

What makes a woman G.I.B? Seriously, I think it is the individual. You may be good to someone, but you may not be good to somebody else.

DOC SEVERINSEN

When I first came to America, a friend suggested that I contact Sybil Leek, the renowned English witch and psychic. Sybil and I talked on the phone and I told her about this book. She had psychic premonitions about its success and she invited me to her home in Florida. Ever since then, Sybil has watched over me with great kindness and friendship. She agreed to be in this book but then she rushed off around the world, leaving me witchless. But I was lucky enough to interview a friend of hers—entertainer and musician Doc Severinsen—when he was appearing at the Sands in Las Vegas. Well-loved by all the millions who watch Johnny Carson nightly, Doc was relaxed, open, and very funny.

The woman who is good in bed is useless if the man she is with doesn't like her. Then being good in bed doesn't keep him with her in any way, unless the man's brains are all in his cock.

The woman who is good in bed is not obvious the moment you meet her, but I think you can get very strong vibrations about whether or not she is going to be good. Some women believe they give off those vibrations of being good in bed, but they don't. I think the type of woman who gives you a straight look in the eyes, has a certain sincerity, and is not exhibitionistic in her behavior is most likely to be good in bed.

The most important thing in telling if a woman is good in bed is looking into her eyes. Everything is in the eyes and in the attitude of a woman's face. If she is relaxed and friendly, she is probably going to be good in bed. Some men think a very sensuous mouth is the answer, others think beauty makes a woman good in bed. But I don't agree that beauty makes a woman better or worse in bed, nor do I think an ugly woman is necessarily going to be better or worse. Of course one can always discuss certain physical criteria like the size of the woman's body, her hair color, the depth of her vagina. I think in some cases a nice, tight pussy is not a bad thing, but the response matters just as much.

My opinion of what is good in bed could change. If a woman is an ideal woman, she will probably be ideal in bed: intelligent, with definite tendencies of a Pisces, and willing to give a man a certain degree of freedom, knowing that if she is taking the right care of him, the home fires will be most appealing. And definitely a woman who is interested in domestic things, and doesn't have to have hired help to do important intimate things like cooking.

A woman who fakes out of bed will usually also fake *in* bed as well. I can spot a real bullshitter, and there's no point in fooling around with anyone like that—whether in bed or out of it. An honest woman is going to be best in bed.

I would rather have a sincere virgin than an insincere hooker who knows every trick. Anyway, I don't see what satisfaction there is in paying for sex, however good the technique is.

Response makes a woman good in bed, and if a response didn't appear, eventually, after a certain amount of time, and the woman didn't have an orgasm with me, I would think I was definitely lacking, and she was. Then I would probably start looking for somebody else, but I don't mean after one evening, because nervous frustration, fear, and physical problems could cause that at first. After all, sex develops. I think many times people who are very compatible, and even in love, can have some very disappointing sexual encounters at first, but they can get a great deal better. Really, though, I would rather have a woman who was interested enough in what I was doing to get a climax fairly soon, and many of them after that.

When you first get into bed the beauty is exploring together and finding out what you both want. I think a sexual relationship between a man and a woman is a brand new voyage. It's a whole new journey, and a lot of interesting things can develop along the way, so you can't go into it with your preconceived opinion: "This is the way I feel about sex, and this is *exactly* what I demand, and this is what I want, and if it doesn't meet with my requirements, then it's no good." A woman should never give a list of what she wants in bed. If she did, I would tell her: "This is not a supermarket, and we don't have orders to take out." Everything should be instinctive; nobody is teaching anybody anything, you are not going to school, and I don't believe sex is something you can learn. Sex is two people sharing a bit of life together.

I am an older man now, but when I was a kid, sex was a different thing. Now, as you get older, there is something else you are looking for in sex: affection and love, as well. A real love affair can develop and grow out of two people that are compatible sexually. There has to be a lot of feeling between them, although it doesn't have to be love at first sight. Being in love has never yet saved any relationship that I know of. There is a constant need for the continuous injection of sex in any relationship, and people don't realize it. They forget that the candlelight must continue to glow, the wine has to keep flowing, because that can get a relationship over some rocky spots and hard times. Clinging to each other in a sexual way at times is never a bad thing. Sex has to be sustained between two people.

When I die, I would like to die in the throes of a sexual embrace with a woman. I would like to be at least eighty-nine years old, and die of ecstasy, in the middle of an orgasm, and all of a sudden I would like to look up and see St. Peter.

MAXIMILIAN SCHELL

What makes a woman G.I.B? Passion and love.

LOVELACE WATKINS

Lovelace Watkins is one of the few entertainers on the Las Vegas Strip who gets a standing ovation in the middle *of his act.*

A woman is good in bed if she is a complete woman, giving her all and desiring to be passionate. If she is satisfied herself, then she is going to satisfy the man. There is no point in trying to formalize it, there are no ground rules—all the emphasis should be on enjoyment. Sex is between two people—both striving to please each other.

A good man makes a woman good. That is, a man who shows care and tenderness, a man who can bring a woman to respond, who cares, shows that he cares, and that he feels it is very important that the woman is also pleased.

There is no such thing as a frigid woman. It depends on the way men treat women. Some men make love quickly, only bother about their own pleasure, and then the sex is over before it has begun. A woman may be inhibited, or maybe hasn't been successful in reaching a climax, but most of the time she just hasn't been exposed to the right man who shows her that he cares.

CLORIS LEACHMAN

What makes a woman G.I.B? You don't need to know tricks.

JACK CARTER

I was confronted by the ultimate journalistic nightmare when I met and interviewed comedian Jack Carter at a party launching Beverly and Vidal Sassoon's bestselling book, A Year of Beauty and Health. *In the middle of his answer, the tape broke. I expected Carter to walk away and follow up later with a distilled version of his original answer, but when I had fixed the tape, he rallied with this funny routine.*

What makes a woman G.I.B? First of all, she must be punctual—she must show up on time. Then she must be naked. That helps. She must say things like "Oooh," "Aaah," and "Ouch," and "Cover me when you're finished," if she is bored. Then she must be clean. Have a washcloth and have a small geisha girl waiting in the glove compartment of your car. But, most important of all, she must be courteous. She must say "Thank you" for the receipt of money or goodies or twenty dollars left on the dresser, and there must always be a drunken maid on the floor yelling, "Nothing for the bridesmaid?" That's it, that's what makes a woman good.

BERNIE CORNFELD

What makes a woman G.I.B? A lot of tenderness, I would think.

MANDY RICE DAVIES

Mandy Rice Davies and Christine Keeler, femmes fatales of the sixties, were notorious for their sexploits with the British aristocracy and particularly Member of Parliament John Profumo. I managed to catch Mandy on a flying visit from her home in Tel Aviv to New York, where she was shooting an Israeli film.

I have faked in bed, and the men were absolutely, completely convinced by my faking. My secret is *not* to make a lot of noise, to be a good actress, and never, never overact. Enjoying sex is being good in bed, but I should think 80 percent of women fake to give the appearance of being good in bed. A woman can be good, in a man's view, yet not enjoy sex—except that never works in the long run. You can fake on a one-night stand, but not in a relationship carried over the years. I don't think women are born good in bed. All that comes later—usually much later in life—if they haven't been spoiled already by faking and not being honest.

If a woman wanted to project her "good in bed" quality, I would always advise her to look non-sexy. Low-cut dresses seem out of date, and looking sexy is a very low-class turn on. I don't think men are turned on in the flesh by overt sex. It is important to be a little more cool if you want to attract a glamorous man. The exploding iceberg bit works far better than looking sexy does. I also think charm is important; charm is the biggest aphrodisiac in the world. But you can't really define it, because some people just are awfully charming because of their smiles, their manners, and their warmth.

Mystery matters in bed. I don't agree with talking a lot in bed, and I don't use words to turn a man on, although it is important for a woman to be able to ask for what she wants in bed. She should always wait for the right opportunity, though. For example, it is easier to make sexual demands on those evenings when two people are very turned on and are at an ideal point in their relationship. But when a woman meets a man for the first time, she should never make demands.

I'm for anything that is basically between two people; as far as oral sex is concerned, I'm in. But I wouldn't like a guy who suggested orgies or threesomes in bed. If I were in love with him, I would probably fall out of love with him immediately. I fall in love with someone I have something in common with; I'm way past the age of falling in love with a man for mysterious reasons. And I am not really interested in anything beyond what happens between two people in bed.

I don't really think the average person wants to cross certain lines, sexually. People still like sexual secrecy. In a magazine there was a cartoon of group sex. Two people were screwing, and the man was saying, "I'll tell my wife I'm working late," and the woman says, "I'll tell my husband I'm going to the movies." In the middle of an orgy where they both could screw quite freely, they still wanted to have secret meetings.

I am not interested in group sex. Once, though, I was invited to a party which turned out to be the only orgy I've ever been to in my life. Somebody answered the door in just his socks. I thought it was a joke and said, "Don't be silly. Put your clothes on." I was embarrassed to admit that I didn't like it. Anyway, recently the girl that gave the orgy wrote an article about me. The orgy was years ago, but I picked up the magazine and read: "Mandy Rice Davies walked into the orgy, took a look around, and walked out, obviously frigid." I loved that.

Kinky sex just doesn't turn me on. I can assure you there has never been anything like sadomasochism in my relationships. The Profumo Affair—it was, how can I describe it?—naive decadence. At the time, though, you see, it sounded awfully out of place. The affairs were perfectly moral, but what happened around them was a little more decadent. But when scandals start snowballing, they gather up everything around. I had had a brief affair with Lord Astor and Douglas Fairbanks, Jr., but none of those involved anything remotely kinky.

I am not as hot as I was made out. People who are given a sexy image often get inhibited. Men sometimes react to a woman with a sexy image quite differently from what you might expect. Men very often don't want to go to bed with me because they are trying to prove that they don't fancy me, or else that they don't want me just for sex.

I had one or two relationships with male movie stars at the time when I was very well-known. We were both incredibly nervous. *I* was nervous because *he* was supposed to have a reputation for being good in bed, and *he* was nervous because *I* was supposed to have a reputation for being good in bed. So, instead of the sex being very hot and heavy, in the end nothing happened at all and we finished off just sitting in bed having coffee and sandwiches.

TONY ORLANDO

What makes a woman G.I.B? I don't keep scorecards.

BARRY WHITE

I have two wishes related to my interview with Barry White: the first is that the tape be set to music, and the second is that I had met all my other interviewees in the same way as superstar singer, writer, composer, arranger, and producer Barry White. Many interviews in this book took months to arrange, but Barry's took me just one minute because I met him totally by accident. I was moving out of my apartment and leaving Los Angeles, and on the last day I ran into Barry White in the corridor. So, after recovering from the surprise, I did an on-the-spot interview:

My woman has to be a perfect woman because I'm a perfectionist. I'm a Virgo. The way that I choose a woman is by her star sign. She has to be one of my signs because I know which signs I like and can relate to. I can get along with any women, but it's whether or not I want to go through the trip with them. I deal in horoscopes and personalities, and I've had every woman in the horoscope—two of each—and their personalities are identifiable by their star signs.

To me, some of the greatest women are Leo women, Gemini women, Libra women, Taurus women, and Capricorn women—it's in their makeup. A true Capricorn woman is feminine; she knows she's feminine, she likes being feminine, and that's what makes her so good. She also can adapt to anything her man wants. Libra women can stay at one balance—they don't change much, which a man likes. Taurus women can flex with a man; they know how to flex. A Taurus woman can take a weak man and make him think he is strong: because of the way she deals with men, she upgrades a man instead of trying to downgrade him until the upgrading becomes outrageous.

The worst thing a woman can do in bed is to be something that she is not—especially with me, because I can tell. Women always overact. I like sex to flow naturally. I am in command because I am a man, so it is important for me to understand, creatively, what I am doing to a woman in bed. I want to know how to do it, to that *particular* woman. There are a lot of men who don't care what they do to a woman, as long as they are satisfied.

It doesn't matter if a woman takes a long time to come. That depends on the man, how much the woman is into him and what he knows. A woman isn't less good if she asks for what she wants in bed; it depends on *how* she asks, and *what* she asks. A woman should always be honest just like a man should, and say what it is, say what she means, and mean what she says. It's in my nature to analyze a conversation with anybody, not just a woman. You meet women who say things like, "I'm not interested in money." That could be true, yet it may not be true. There are times when it isn't so. I like to find out the truth.

Women are very gullible. They see Barry White and they fall apart. They should never do that, because I'm a human being like the rest of the men. The only difference is that I have a job which keeps me in front of a lot of other women. Women always want something that another woman wants. They can't help that, but they should try to control it and be honest.

There isn't any special age group of women who are good in bed. I've seen women of nineteen be equally good as women of forty-five. But there's no doubt about it, love makes a woman good in bed. I know so. The women that don't have it are very miserable, and the ones that do are very happy.

I don't get hung up on the things that other men get hung up on. They get hung up on a woman's looks and what she has got on, then they want to go to bed with her. Men meet a woman and think she is so beautiful that no matter what is wrong with her personality, "I'll go along with it." Well, I am not that way. Shit, no! I don't give a fuck how a woman looks—if she ain't together, it's over, there's nothing to talk about. I can usually tell by talking to a woman, by having a conversation with her, what she is basically looking for, sexually, because me, when I am talking to a woman, I just talk to her, I am listening to what she is saying, analyzing what she is saying. Then I can tell what she wants in life, how she looks at life, how she faces problems every day.

Refusing what she doesn't want in bed is the prerogative of a woman. After all, she is an individual. A lot of men try to take that from women—being an individual. Me, I like to enhance it. If I find a woman who has a beautiful personality and is a beautiful person, I don't subtract from it and I don't add to it. In any case, everybody's opinion of what makes a woman good in bed has to be different, because everybody doesn't see the same person in the same way.

ROBERT MITCHUM

What makes a woman G.I.B? Proximity.

BO HOPKINS

Blond, slow-talking Southerner Bob Hopkins first made an impact as the hard-nosed leader of the Pharaohs in American Graffiti *and since then in his many TV and film roles.*

I am horny and lustful, like everybody else, but I am a little choosy. I don't want to lie in bed with someone I am not responding to, who is not responding to me. Beauty has got nothing to do with being good in bed, though, of course, I am not going to turn down a beautiful girl. You have to find out. I have dated girls who were absolutely beautiful, but they were just like cookies in the bakery. They looked good until you bit down on them; then you discovered they weren't good at all. I went out with a model from New York. She was very beautiful. She was a lot of talk until we got in bed. Then she was very, very stiff. That's being bad in bed.

I was twelve when my mother told me about sex, and I remember her telling me things I already knew. Then she still didn't tell me everything. My parents and my grandmother, who taught Sunday school, told me that sex was bad—that masturbation was bad, and I'd go crazy; that girls could get me in trouble. Yet at night I could hear my aunts and uncles pounding away—"Oh, God, oh, God"—and I kept saying, "Why is it so bad? *They* sound as if they are having a good time."

Society is hypocritical, and I am against it. It put a lot of shit in my head that don't make no sense. I was told that sex was bad, and that I had to go to church and listen to a preacher tell me that hellfire and damnation would get me, but all the while, that same preacher was out screwing little choir girls. That's bullshit. But that's what I grew up with, and I fought it. That's why I was in reform school three times.

I had a relationship with a teacher when I was twelve years old, which I couldn't tell anybody about. She probably taught me more about sex than anybody else; she was thirty, very gentle and very nice, and she taught me things I didn't even know existed. I wanted to tell everyone about it, because all the other boys wanted to lay her, but I knew if I did, I would ruin a good thing.

I went with a prostitute for one and a half years. We were both sixteen, and I was in the service. She was working in a house in Port Arthur, Texas, and she was beautiful, I never questioned her about what she did.

In the South, we are brought up to say "Yes, ma'am" and "No, ma'am," so when I went to New York and found out that the girl was the aggressor, I was very surprised. I had never known that before. I met a girl there who was good in bed and used psychology on me. I'd come off the set, tired, not in the mood even though I'm horny, but when I come in, I'm shaving, and she's rubbing my back, and she's wearing a sexy dress. And pretty soon I am saying "Let's go to bed," whereas, when I came in, I wasn't thinking about sex. But when we did it, it was beautiful. I felt better, and there was tension release.

I went with a beautiful Argentinian girl for three and a half years. She was dark haired—a little like Ava Gardner. She was married to a psychiatrist and I was in love with her. It was the first time I was ever in love.

She was great in bed. I think in each man's life two or three women like that come along. And when a third one comes along, you'd better grab her. She was the first woman I ever climaxed with four times in one night—the first time I got her into bed I said, "Hey, I've got to see you at least once a week." Soon it was every night. I couldn't be without her, but we didn't have sex every night; just being with her was very sexy, very sensual.

She was great. Every time I went to bed with her, it was a different experience, even though it was the same experience. I couldn't bear to be separated from her. She was beautiful, intelligent, and very sensual and sexy. She could get along with truck drivers, yet she could talk to the Queen of England. She knew how to please me, knew all of my vulnerable spots, and when I was down, she brought me up. She always made sure that I felt great. Sometimes I would make her come five or six times and didn't climax at all myself. For me, that's love.

Sex is different for everyone. Sex is like love. I can say it in a Southern accent; I can say it in a New York accent; I can say it in a French accent. That's what makes the world go round. That's why you meet some people that say, "Hey, lay it on me," that's beautiful. And then you meet other girls that say, "Oh, I've never done it before." I've done the same. I don't like lies, but I have made a woman feel sorry for me, because once in a while when a girl feels sorry for you, I know it's the easiest way to get her into bed.

Since I've come to Hollywood, lots of quirks and things I've never heard of have happened; I don't like a woman who is very aggressive, and I've had a chick come up to me at a party and say, "Let's fuck." All I said was, "Well, pick another time." I think a lot of women would still rather the man was the aggressor. I don't mean throw her down and knock her out. Although if I'm drunk and a girl comes up to me and says, "Let's fuck," that's her problem, because I might just do it. I don't mind a woman saying, "Gee, Bo, you are cute," and things like that which make sense, but nothing too aggressive.

Another thing I don't like is vulgarity in a woman. That turns me off. But if, when we're banging around in a fit of passion and we're both feeling animalistic, the woman says, "Fuck me, Bo, fuck me," you'd better believe I'm damn well going to do it. That's not vulgar—that's human nature. I like a woman to talk. I like her to get aroused and hot, because that makes me go that much more.

Sometimes I get moods. I guess we all have a little sadisticness in us, and I get a little animalistic sometimes. Other times I get very loving, and want to sit and talk about the stars, where I was born, and myself. But really I am in bed to make love, and to make it pleasurable. But before I can screw a girl in the first place, I have to like the hell out of her. Because otherwise I can just get myself a rubber doll. Of course, not everybody need be in love—it can just be infatuation.

I think women have this thing about keeping their virtue, and worrying, "If he gets me into bed tonight, he won't ever want to see me anymore." But that's not always true. Supposing the *guy* isn't good in bed—then the woman may not want to see *him* again. But I still have brought up my daughter to be virtuous and tell her that although sex isn't a dirty thing, and there's absolutely nothing wrong with it, I would rather she wait until she is married. Every father hopes that. It's only natural. If I had a son, I would say, "Get as much experience as you can"—but I can't say the same to my daughter.

I know that's unfair, but that's society. And I know that if my daughter one time puts out in high school, then breaks up with the guy, he is going to tell all the other guys. Then they will go out with her not because of her, but because she screwed this other guy, so sooner or later it will be all over school that she lays on her back and she fucks. It's wrong—I know it's wrong—but what can I do? I don't want my daughter to be labeled. I don't want her to get hurt. She knows all about sex—I've prepared her. I've shown her dirty books and dirty pictures, so she'll be prepared. Pictures of sixty-nine positions, and all those things, so she'll be prepared.

In a moment of weakness, though, I'll look at the fifteeen- or sixteen-year-old girls who sometimes come around when I'm on location, and I've almost been caught. Then I'll look at them and I'll say, "Geez, my daughter's that age."

A lot of things make a woman good in bed. Some women

are very intelligent in bed; they make a man feel good. They caress him and talk to him very soft and very low. They're very sexy. The way they take off their clothes is very seductive. To me a woman is more sensuous and I get more sexed up when she is in panties and bra than I do when I see her naked because *I've* had nothing to do with that. I'd rather walk into a room, find her with all her clothes on, then slowly get them off.

No inhibitions make a woman good in bed. A lot of women think that when they go down on a man, or he goes down on her, that they are doing a perversion. What is a perversion? I don't know. Do you know that it is against the law in California to go down on your wife? That's bullshit. Perversion to me is someone who messes with my kid, or out-and-out rapes someone. Anything else is whatever you want. Although I am not into, well, I better not say, I might meet a girl that is; in fact I did three weeks ago for the first time in my life, but I am never too much into the sodomy thing. It hurts me and I don't know how the hell the girl feels.

A woman should enjoy sex. It doesn't matter if it takes her a long time to come. She should enjoy it for what it is. I don't think she should put a time schedule on sex. I don't think a man who is really into sex cares if a woman takes a long time to come. If she enjoys sex and it takes fifteen minutes, that's what counts. If she enjoys sex and it takes two hours, that's what counts. If she enjoys sex and it takes a day and a half, that's what counts. I don't think you should put any time or any labels on sex—just enjoy it.

JOE NAMATH

What makes a woman G.I.B? My mother doesn't allow me to talk about sex.

BIANCA JAGGER

Bianca Jagger and I sat on the floor of the Jaggers' Chelsea house, ate Chinese food, and talked all night. I had phoned Bianca earlier that evening, knowing that she was in London for the Stones concert at Knebworth, and had asked her to do this interview. She was uncertain, but she said that in any case she wanted to read my manuscript. So I arranged to have it delivered to her and to meet her later that evening.

I expected to find a cold, remote beauty living in the outlandish world of Pop; instead, I found Bianca in white pajamas. with no makeup, stunning, warm, feminine, and intelligent. And the only wayout element in our interview was that it began at midnight and ended at dawn.

I need to be flirtatious; I am what the French call *une allumeuse;* I like to light every fire possible. Because I feel I behave in a very manly way, even being very feminine physically and in my behavior, my mind is manly, so sometimes I feel insecure and I need to feel that maybe men find me attractive. I'm always scared that when people meet me they will either think that I am frigid or that I am capable of doing anything. But in fact I am very romantic, not conservative, but shy. I feel that I have not experienced—I don't believe in all the tricks—I am completely vulnerable, as if I were thirteen. In a way, I suppose, each time a woman goes to bed with a man she is a little bit of a virgin.

I was brought up in a very feudal society; my parents were very puritanical, so I was brought up to believe that you remain a virgin until you marry a man. You could not be presented to marry someone if you were not a virgin. You asked me if I was ever scared to refuse something in bed. Well, I was brought up to believe that so many things should be refused, even within marriage. When I was a little girl we had lessons at school and I heard about all the things that were "accepted within wedlock" and all the things that were not. Natural things were accepted—unnatural things were not. And I always wondered what the hell natural things were—and for years after I still believed some things were "natural."

Thirteen years of convent [life] do not go away in one minute; no matter what you do, they are still there. I think I have a lot of guilt about sex deep, deep inside my subconscious, even if my intelligence refuses to accept it. But then some studies of women show that guilt is very, very important for sexual satisfaction—that a woman who has no guilt whatsoever just does it like having lunch or playing tennis. I sometimes admire a woman who is capable of having sexual relations with a man just because she wants him sexually. But I am incapable of doing that; I can't just go and meet somebody and say, "Well, why not?"

When I was still a virgin I went to live in France. I felt so vulnerable, such a little girl, so inexperienced and naive. Being a virgin was so peculiar at that time in Paris. I was so scared—I thought, "What would a man do?" I always used to feel inferior to the other girls because I was a virgin and they had affairs and were free. Then one day I realized that being free is not doing everything that is available to you, but eliminating all the things you don't want to do and waiting for the one you do want. People who are free don't need to prove anything. Freedom is to be able to say to a man, "I don't want to fuck you,'' because I either want to be on my own, or I love somebody to whom I want to be faithful.

But a lot of men try to make you feel insecure if you refuse them. They say, ''Are you frigid?'' or that maybe you don't feel anything, maybe you are not sensual, maybe you are not sexual. They think if they accuse you of being frigid you will go to bed with them. That happened a lot when I was an adolescent in Paris. And maybe because I first started to be a woman in France—always, even today, I feel like a little girl when I am there—and Frenchmen always make me feel insecure. Every time a Frenchman asks me to have a cup of coffee I still feel like a virgin, as if I couldn't cope and wouldn't know what to do if he made a pass at me.

An Englishman can invite you to have a cup of tea in his house—he will offer you a cup of tea—then, if it happens, it happens. But a Frenchman will invite you to his house and tell you to come and have breakfast with croissants. Not only will he expect you to go to bed with him, but he will probably expect you to make breakfast as well. And if you refuse to go to bed with him, he will find a reason to hurt you—will become intent on making you feel you're not a woman of the world, and are unsophisticated or frigid.

Nowadays I say, ''Am I supposed to be frigid because I don't want to fuck you?'' Or I say, ''I couldn't,'' or ''I feel so tired,'' or, ''Mick . . .'' Being married is a marvelous asset, you know, and people accept it very willingly. Except sometimes they say, ''Oh, well, I thought you were more *en vogue* and free. You are really so bourgeois.'' But it's not important what other people think, it's what you know about yourself.

I was in love for a long, long time with a man who was much older than me. He made me feel secure, had tolerance. I wanted protection, I wanted affection, I wanted tenderness and someone who was not the kind of person who didn't care what

I felt, what I wanted, or who just wanted to take me. I was always afraid of making love to a man who made me feel as if I was being taken, of a man who did not share anything with me, but was making love to a reflection of himself, as if one was an object that reflected his own image—but had no contact with him. Not an exchange, but being with someone who looks at you as if you were transparent.

I hate the idea of being taken unless I decide that I want to be taken, and I only decide that when I know that the man is willing to give himself and when there's no longer a relationship of power. I am fascinated by power—but I am terrified if somebody else exerts it over me. Power is the great game between men and women which men think they have won—but that is not true because the greatest power over a politician, creative artist, and an intellectual was always the secret power women have. Someone once said that the power women have over men is when they discover a man's weakness and then reassure him.

A woman's secret power is not just being good in bed. Everybody is a potential great lover—unless they are physically insensitive. Every man can make a woman into a great lover, and every woman can make a man into a great lover. But I don't believe being good in bed has anything to do with techniques. It's to do with love, with emotions, tenderness, and intellect. It is also to do with the freedom a man makes you feel, the tenderness you see in him, and the confidence he gives you because confidence makes you daring. You dare to do things with someone who makes you feel confident about yourself, about your behavior, about your morals. A woman is sometimes afraid to be sexually free because she thinks, "If I was really myself and really show what I want sexually and sensually, maybe he will underestimate me and think I am some kind of a tart."

You shouldn't have to ask for what you want in bed. I hate

words. I think that if you have any amount of communication and understanding, you don't need to use words unless the man is selfish and assumes there are things that are due to him and not to the woman. I would advise a woman to be with a man who gives her tenderness. And an intellectual woman should be with a man she has respect for. To be sexually turned on by someone I need, to a certain extent, to have respect and esteem for him. Otherwise, sexually, he wouldn't interest me whatsoever. If I don't respect the person, he becomes nonexistent to me.

I think the obsession with orgasm is a great problem in our society. A great deal of sexual dissatisfaction is due to the fact that people think the orgasm is so essential. If you study old civilizations like the Incas and the Egyptians, you find that the period before the orgasm is what is important. I don't believe in faking; being truthful matters in bed, and I don't fake. I think one shouldn't only when you try to avoid pain for somebody you love.

When you love somebody you want to give them as much pleasure as you can. People talk about marvelous Japanese girls who know every sexual secret and then one feels so limited. When you really love somebody you feel so jealous of somebody else who is able to give them more pleasure than you did. I would never really dare ask a man if I was good in bed. But when I meet a man who is successful (I am very fascinated by people that have success—I sometimes feel I should be ashamed of liking success and people who have it) you feel so insecure because there you stand and you think they must have known some extraordinary woman that was so beautiful, so intelligent, maybe so marvelous in bed. And that is why I always want to say, "Who is the woman, what did she do that maybe I could do, how was she that maybe I could be better?"

So I ask them, "Who was the woman that you thought was

sexually the greatest?" And then they pretend and say, "Of course you," and then I say, "I wasn't asking about me." Anyway, you feel they're lying because you always think there was somebody more extraordinary physically, that there was somebody more sensually free, more experienced. You always think that even when you believe they really desire you, when you feel they're really touched by you and really moved by you, that maybe in their mind there is still a myth—somebody else they loved and desired that you will never ever be able to surpass.

I have felt incredibly, incredibly unconfident—you can walk into a room, feel you're fantastic and everybody looks at you, but you know that still doesn't mean anything when you're really close to a man. Because he can feel, "She is so beautiful, but anyway I don't want her." Or he can want a beautiful woman to own like you own beautiful objects or you own beautiful paintings. Being beautiful, being glamorous, and looking wonderful does not mean that a man will want you. Being beautiful and being good in bed alone won't satisfy a person.

I have talked about emotions and tenderness, but it is passion that is extraordinary. Passion is part of your character—some women are born passionate. Passion is being able to make love to a person and go beyond life and into death. For me fantasy is so much more important than reality. My dream—I am so romantic that for me the greatest thing will always be a book by Saint Exupery called *The Little Prince*. I shouldn't say it (because he is so arrogant) but when I met Mick he became for me the Little Prince and the rest was part of reality, but with him it was all part of fantasy. When you get that with somebody who can talk fantasy, then the rest doesn't matter.

Until Mick the search was for a father figure—for the protection and affection a father can provide. And the day I think I grew up a little bit—the day I didn't need a father figure any more—was when I fell in love with Mick because he was my older brother—he was no longer the father.

Mick taught me that being vulnerable and needing somebody and loving somebody and being able to say that is not weak. Before Mick I was incapable of that. I never thought somebody could want, need, and be dependent on somebody without losing their dignity. Mick taught me that because he is capable of doing it without ever losing his dignity. People think that if they are capable of being vulnerable they will lose their dignity. One almost never dares say thing like, "I need you, I love you." A real relationship is when one is capable of saying that, while always keeping your dignity and nevertheless with the understanding that if the person didn't want you, you wouldn't want them any more—because you like yourself.

I do feel threatened by other women wanting Mick, but you could feel threatened with any man, because they are all human. No matter who he is, he may turn a corner tomorrow and find a woman he thinks much more extraordinary than the one he has at home. But that's the risk everybody in the world has, every man and every woman. But if things are going to be ended, they are going to be ended anyway. The intelligent thing is not to think about how insecure you should be, but try to be balanced within the situation. You have to have something with somebody beyond sex and physique and success, something very, very special that goes beyond all the superficial and trivial things, that gives you the feeling that you have something with somebody that nobody else has, something timeless. Being good in bed is not timeless.

MARTY ALLEN

What makes a woman G.I.B? The right man.

GENE WILDER

Gene Wilder is the brilliant comedy star of movies like The Producers *and* Blazing Saddles, *and the director, writer, and star of* Sherlock Holmes' Smarter Brother.

My strongest feeling is that the more things revert to sexual technique, or what makes someone good or bad, the more it leads to the destruction of the natural impulses that make a woman good. The very question insults me. Not that it shouldn't be asked, but when it *is* asked, everyone should realize there is no answer—no A, B, C, or D—that makes a woman good in bed.

The strongest force working for sexual pleasure any time I have made love to a woman was when an honest affection existed between that woman and myself. And I am almost incapable of making love with a woman for just a quick bang—as it is called—however beautiful the woman, or however instantaneously the passing fancy took me. If I did that, I know not only would the experience be unsatisfactory, but also the event would leave me less than I was before. When there is an affection—I don't say that you have to be in love—when the guards are let down, then the desire to touch and hold overcomes the pounding of the heart.

Just as in acting there is no right way to do a scene, there is no right way to make love. With one woman the criteria would be completely different than with another woman—with different factors making them both good. Some women do things in bed that make you say, "She made me feel so good and I hope I made her feel good." But then with another woman it didn't matter at all if the same things were done or left undone.

Sex is relating to the woman for what she is, and the woman relating to you for what she feels—not having a standard supposed to show off the man's expert technique in lovemaking. There is no such thing as good in bed. That is a fallacy. Good is if you are happy with someone.

TONY BENNETT

What makes a woman G.I.B? Coming together.

BOB GUCCIONE

Forum, Penthouse, *and* Viva *are in the forefront of debates on sex and sexuality. I interviewed their creator, Bob Guccione.*

Most women are good in bed in some respect. There have been a variety of great women in my life who have all been good for different reasons. Some were enthusiastic oral types—adventurous and probing. Then there were other women who felt incredible. Their skin, their body heat, was completely different from any I had ever felt before.

There are some women who, when you fuck them, make you feel you are being sucked off at the same time. They seem to envelop you totally with a kind of warmth which they generate in their skin. It's what the French call "a question of skin." Then there are other women who resemble the stereotype and *seem* better in bed because they're so idealized—long legged, a tiny waist, beautiful firm buttocks, and big firm tits.

Another kind of woman whom I adore is excitingly vulgar in bed, hungrily sensual, who makes a lot of noise when she eats you. It is a facet of her sensuality and it makes her interesting and exceptional. There are some women who are submissive, in a very nice way, and satisfy yet another strange need by enslaving themselves to you. And there are still other women who play a dominant role. A woman is more likely to be good sexually if she is concerned with her body. All of these different women have different specialized sexual interests and as a result of these specialized interests they are exceptional in bed.

The type of woman who is good in bed is good regardless of her looks. She usually has much greater personal magnetism than other women, no matter how beautiful they are.

Girls who are very beautiful, who become top models, top film stars, grow up very differently than ordinary girls. It is by virtue of their great beauty that they are admired and stared at and lusted after from the earliest age: they're constantly pursued, so they develop mutated values. A beautiful woman knows her physical beauty gains her attention, and she will have been made to believe, by actual *experience*, that being beautiful is more than sufficient—in bed or out of it. She doesn't think she needs any intelligence, poise, or personality because she has always been singled out. So she feels that it is enough for a man to see her private parts. That's all that's necessary on her part.

The woman who *is* good has had to fight for every bit of attention she ever got. She is a woman with a big ego who demands it—and needs a lot of attention. That type of woman will be infinitely better in bed because she is used to working at giving satisfaction in one form or another. In bed, when she is meeting a serious interpersonal challenge, she will use her other assets faster than the woman who is beautiful.

The prime ingredient for a woman to be good in bed is enthusiasm. If she is enthusiastic, she's going to be great, even if she's clumsy. But enthusiasm can't be taught—it has got to be a reflection of the dynamic interest of the woman.

A woman who is good in bed is aware, not just of the man's needs, but of her own needs and abilities. She is very experimental in her own right—seeks new dimensions of satisfaction. But, however experimental she is, when you meet her, she is still a little shy. Women who come on very strong, very bold, and are apparently very up-front sexually are usually not very good in bed. I don't trust anyone, man or woman, who makes a lot of discussing sex, unless the atmosphere or the situation calls for that type of discussion.

A man who is really sexy, really good in bed, may show the woman how to do certain things. More important than that, he encourages her. The woman who is good in bed is not good with every man; even a prostitute with a highly polished technique applies that technique differently from individual to individual and is always influenced by the encouragement she gets from the man.

People perform best against feedback, against reception. It's like a comedian who stands up in front of an audience and tells a few jokes. If he doesn't get any laughs, he feels that the house is cold and he is not going to perform well. If, on the other hand, he tells his first few jokes and has the house in stitches, that is obviously going to loosen him up. He will be sharper and faster, because an atmosphere and an environment have been created which are conducive to his performance—just like a couple in bed.

True sexual satisfaction is a two-way thing. If I went to bed with a woman who turned me on, whom I admired, but who wasn't really very good, I would *make* her good by virtue of the integrity of my feelings, my own needs, and my interest. That interest helps me to know the kind of woman I am in bed with; then I know how to direct my efforts.

You have to penetrate a woman's defenses. Getting into her

head is a prerequisite to getting into her body. Once I get into her head, I do everything, say everything, and act in every way according to my particular sensitivity—my ability to understand what that woman is and what she needs. Fulfilling the needs of the woman he is in bed with makes a *man* good in bed. If I were asked for a one-line answer to the question, "What makes a woman good in bed?" I would say, "A man who is good in bed."

BRENDA VACCARO

What makes a woman G.I.B? Don't you know a woman never really knows if she is good. It's just magic, there is no clue. There is no such thing as good in bed; you should never open your eyes and never say anything—there is no way to explain good.

ISAAC HAYES

Isaac Hayes, Academy Award-winning superstar of sexy soul music, did this interview at his house in Coldwater Canyon in California.

The ideal woman for me would be a superwoman in bed—a woman who is very, very long-winded and can make love for hours, especially when my appetite is sharp. She must be able to please me with foreplay to the point of almost uncontrollable desire. She must be creative, with a lot of imagination, so she is capable of being different things—for example, more or less like a slave sometimes. A woman who is very uninhibited, who would say, do, or feel anything that she wanted to during sex, including oral sex—the whole trip. A woman with endurance, with a lot of fire, with warmth, uninhibited, and of course, a good-looking body—that helps.

There are some women who are physically perfect—not body-wise, but in their genital area: the texture and the location of the vaginal canal. Not necessarily tightness; it can be the fatty tissues in the walls of the vagina that add a lot. Also the erotic juices and the secretion of those juices and the overall feel. Sometimes a woman doesn't have to move at all, and can produce an orgasm from a man just effortlessly, whereas others have to work and do all kinds of things, yet still do not get the same results out of a man as the ones with that natural feel.

Vibrations and a sixth sense can detect if a woman is good in bed. I guess you could say my sensuous antenna might be outstretched, and it could pick up some radiations from a woman. I've been deceived sometimes by women, though; some I would expect great things of and was disappointed, yet with others I wasn't expecting great things, but was pleasantly surprised.

I find the more common-looking or unattractive women are much better in bed than the very, very attractive women. It seems as if beautiful women are too hung up on their outward appearance. Whereas the woman who is not so attractive and knows that all she has is herself and her body is not inhibited by, "I wonder if I will get my makeup running down my face, or my hair will get messed up." The unattractive woman doesn't care about that and just gets totally involved and expresses herself. But if you do find a woman who is attractive *and* good in bed, she is dynamite.

I always select the woman who is stand-offish—who seems

to be shy, not trying to catch my eye with avoiding glances. Because you find that the women that are all upfront, wow, waving flags and stuff, are very shallow and are trying to do a sales job on you—and I bypass those.

Whereas the woman that seems to be shy, not too extraverted, will attract me. Somehow or other I will get to her, get her attention.

Then there are women that seem to be very confident. If I am in the mood for a challenging situation, I like the woman who is very confident and looks as if she is saying, "I am just as important to me as you are." If she values herself, then she must *be* of some value. Evidently people have reacted to her that way. There had to have been some experiences to justify her attitude of confidence, so then I want that one, too.

A lot of guys expect too much. They expect a woman to be ready-made and responsive. I think women adjust to a man—so you have to get them prepared for your way of lovemaking; that is why there are some inexperienced women who I enjoy more than an experienced woman, because an inexperienced woman can personally adapt herself to me, to my way of lovemaking. Then she discovers new things and her response is so sincere and so honest. The inexperienced woman is so open—she can bend either way, like a young sapling. If, again, the man is sharp and adept, he can mold her in a way that will please him. But, of course, the experienced woman also has her way of doing things and of pleasing the man.

It's up to the man to put a woman in such a mental state that he will have complete control of her physical faculties. Then he can get what he wants out of her. It doesn't matter to me how long it takes a woman to come, because after a while you know if she is frequently orgasmic or if she is infrequently orgasmic. Then you can just build according to the way she wants you to. You can tell by her body language, by her reaction in bed. Then, after several sexual involvements with her, you should really know where to take her.

Some women are multiple-orgasmic; I have known women (I have counted for my own satisfaction) within a ten-hour period to average about fifty orgasms. Then there are those who can only stand one—they are so sensitive that you have to wait so many minutes. The orgasms that take a long time to reach are much stronger than the ones reached quickly, because so much tension and build-up has occurred, so when the woman comes, it just explodes; it's violently strong.

There are some women who are almost totally frigid, with so many mental hang-ups due to the formative years of their maturing, and almost nothing can be done about it. The woman who is bad in bed is very dry, has no juices, very little secretions. She doesn't move, doesn't respond, and is too bashful or ashamed to respond to you.

In the past a woman was supposed to be a lady at all times, even in bed—which is a taboo that cursed a lot of marriages, causing men to drift and look for pleasure elsewhere. And so a lot of guys turn to hookers, because they are uninhibited. Whereas the wife—after it's done—jumps up and washes, and never utters another word until the next day at the breakfast table.

I feel that a woman should be free to say, feel, and do whatever she wants. A sexual experience should be total and completely free. Sometimes a woman will not do something because she is afraid of what the man will think of her. So I think that the man should really tell the woman up front, "Hey, whatever you want to do, you tell me—you tell me what you want me to do, whatever you do is all right."

Women should ask for what they want and not expect a man to be a know-it-all. Sex should be a mutual thing of communication where both partners can exchange different ideas and different feelings and thoughts. Both involved should strive for mutual satisfaction, so there should also be mutual investment of exchange of knowledge and of interest.

I have found that if a woman refuses something in bed, she can be a challenge. Then I make suggestions sometimes and the woman says, "No, I don't want to do that." So I say, "You don't know what you are missing." And she says, "Well, I will never know." But then I keep working on it and I take another approach—sneak up on her blind side, so before she realizes it, she is enjoying what she said she wouldn't do. After a while she really gets to like it and even becomes aggressive with it. So later on, when you talk about it, she says, "Wow, just think what I have been missing."

I feel that with a woman I can cover three hundred and sixty degrees of activities from one extreme to another—from a sadistic to a masochistic attitude. Some women like you to be very warm and tender—which I can be—a woman like that can arouse me by being very warm and tender. Other women like you to be very, very sadistic and violent with them in bed—which I can be also.

Chatter in bed really turns me on. The more a woman talks and really lets me know how she feels, the more it arouses me, because to utter vulgarities is sometimes a turn-on. Also, another thing which turns me on are the natural body odors which generate between two people. They are quite stimulating—not unhygienic, but the ones that arise out of the actual excitement and the activity.

I have experienced sex with women all over the world and I find that Latin women are very torrid, uninhibited lovers. There are good lovers of all races, but I guess I lean toward the exotic: the Oriental, Filipino, Hawaiian, Mexican, and of course, the Black woman.

Basically, the Black woman is what I have known all my life, and for me she is best in bed. I find that in the past decade Black women have become more free with their sexual activities. One thing that I really appreciate about the Black woman is her physical makeup, especially in her genital area, where it's very strong—with the durability to withstand and endure sex. A lot of women of other nationalities are weak, and after a very healthy session they pain or sometimes might even spot. But a Black woman is very strong, and I guess you can look at it hereditarily: working in the fields, having a baby, and then getting up the next day and going back to work.

JAN-MICHAEL VINCENT

What makes a woman G.I.B? Feeling.

GEORGE CHAKIRIS

George Chakiris and I share the same birth sign, and I met him on my twenty-fourth birthday in London. We had tea in his apartment opposite the Albert Hall, and talked about Chopin, the part he was playing in "Notorious Woman." Later, we met again in California, and talked again for hours, this time not about Chopin, but about sex.

The most incredible woman I ever had in bed was so marvelously open and honest about her feelings for me. She was a married woman on the verge of a divorce. Everything was romantic, because the affair was so secretive and we were in Paris and Rome. She said something to me that I have never forgotten: that there was something special about the way we were physically constructed which satisfied us both.

Looks do matter, because one is initially attracted by what one sees. But people put on such facades, so I can't tell if a woman is good in bed by just looking at her. Attractiveness is nothing without the woman being loving—unless you are just out for sex—because then all one needs is a change. Otherwise I think a woman is good in bed because of our feelings for one another.

I don't expect to be terrific the first time that I am with someone, nor that she has to be. Sex develops and becomes good as you discover how to please each other. You become uninhibited. The trouble with sex is that women have always thought they had to be passive and men aggressive, but they should show their different qualities, because both are passive and aggressive at different times and should try and eliminate stereotypes.

We must allow each other to change. If I am with a girl who suddenly does something aggressive, I don't think, "My God, she must be a hooker." Some men won't let their wives do things which they think are perfectly all right for a hooker to do—they allow a hooker to be aggressive because that is her job. Also, some women feel they are cheap if they are aggressive in bed—but that is not true. I think it is a shame that people have problems with sex, because it is such a marvelous thing.

DAVID JANSSEN

What makes a woman G.I.B? I suppose it's in the minds of the two people participating.

GERMAINE GREER

I have always admired Germaine Greer's book, The Female Eunuch, *and I was hoping to get a full length interview with her, but the only chance I had was five minutes after a lecture she gave at the University of Southern California.*

You can't really be serious about this question. I suspect you're suffering from "California brain." I don't understand what "good in bed" means, and I don't know that I have heard men use the phrase. I find the phrase offensive, and I also find offensive the assumption that sex is something that occurs in bed, and not other places. Trying to be a hip fuck is all Dutch to me.

One of the things wrong with the "jockcratic" society is the assumption that sex is a form of athletics. Sex in the seventies has a Puritanism about it. Everybody has intravaginal intercourse.

In some studies that have been done in the past, it has emerged that Black men and Chicano men give head much more often than white men, and your WASP has got a kind of reversed puritanism. On the one hand he condemns polymorphous sexual activity for other groups like gay people, and when it comes to his sexuality, he is more boring (in both senses of the word) than he has ever been before, because now he doesn't have to practice any of the relative perversions to avoid pregnancy, because the woman is medicated to the eyeballs. He just has intravaginal intercourse. Anal intercourse and coitus interruptus and cunnilingus and fellatio are in abeyance, and you won't find much fellatio in Missouri.

I have always assumed that what really seduced people is the degree of communication that they establish. That's all—and also that what makes a woman good in bed is the same as what makes a man good.

ROD STEIGER

What makes a woman G.I.B? Her love and knowledge that she is one-half of what she is going to make happy.

FIONA LEWIS

Strikingly blue-eyed Fiona Lewis starred in Ken Russell's Lisztomania, *has co-starred with Richard Burton and Oliver Reed, and has worked with Roman Polanski.*

I make a good shepherd's pie—but being good in bed? I don't know. The line, "Is she good in bed?"—as one man says to another—is so pathetic because a woman who is supposedly good in bed for one man might be a disaster for another.

It sounds corny, I know, but I think sex is a matter of chemistry and some sort of vibration. Because why do you instantly dislike someone when they walk into a room? Why do you feel instantly sexually attracted to someone else? It must be chemistry, some animalistic thing that has been handed down through the centuries—that you are basically of the same type, of the same breed. You might be a masochist, always wanting to be treated badly; sadism and masochism go together, and so I think that underneath, you are attracted to someone who is really you.

Sex is still terribly new; thirty years ago people didn't live together like they do today. You got married. Everything has accelerated very fast, and it is ridiculous to expect sex and relationships without marriage to work out in the space of thirty years. Even when I was eighteen there was still a certain amount of guilt attached to premarital sex, so you did it secretly and hoped that Mummy didn't find out. But, after having heard for eighteen years of one's life that sex was horrible and awful—it was difficult to get rid of guilt and suddenly turn into Miss-liberated-wonderful-sexual-thing.

Initially, sex was like everything else new. You didn't want to make a fool of yourself; just as when you learned to ride a bicycle, you didn't want to fall off. Also—you didn't know how sex would affect you. It was rather like somebody of sixteen drinking their first bottle of Scotch and taking a long time before discovering if one glass makes them drunk, or three or four. I remember thinking, "What are you supposed to do to be good in bed? What is the magic formula? Do I have to swing from a chandelier? Is there a secret?" How were you to know, having never had sex before? There was no one to compare notes with because women rarely talk about what they do in bed. And very few men will take the trouble to explain that there *is* no secret.

Gradually you realize that being good doesn't really matter at all, and that sex should be a selfish act. Women are much more prone to worry about the man not enjoying himself. Each partner should have as best a time as they can. It's not necessary to keep consulting each other. You don't say, "I want . . ." and then make a list.

All sexual relationships start and end in the mind. It is very difficult to separate the sex act from everything else. I often find that when a relationship wanes, part of the reason is you are no longer enamoured of somebody's mental outlook; they no longer interest you to talk to, and that stage often arrives long before you stop fucking. Something changes mentally before the rest of the relationship goes down the drain; you don't find situations where people have wonderful relationships and the fucking suddenly stops.

The mind can make a woman seem good—but it can also

prevent her from enjoying sex. Sex is an animalistic act, and sometimes it is difficult switching your mind off after a busy day. If you are thinking of the shopping list, you won't relax. If women worry about the time it takes them to have an orgasm (a major problem for most women) or they worry about what the man would like them to do, the chances are that they will do everything wrong, or that the man won't care anyway.

A woman should feel relaxed enough in bed to say and do whatever she wants. A lot of people don't admit being uptight in bed; ideally, there should be a lot of communication between both partners. You should be as relaxed in bed as you are when you watch TV.

GEORGE PEPPARD

What makes a woman G.I.B? I suppose it is the way she feels about men.

OMAR SHARIF

Omar Sharif s dedication to bridge is renowned, and I met him when he was in London for a few days playing in the Evening Standard *Bridge Tournament. Even though he had been playing for most of the day in an intense, smoky atmosphere, Omar immediately agreed to do this interview. We talked the next morning in his Mayfair hotel.*

A woman has to be interested in my body. There are ways of touching that are important to me. I like the feeling of touching very much. Some girls don't, and they are not good for me.

The woman who is good makes you want to have her all the time; she is a woman I want to touch all the time; so I can't keep my hands off her, and she likes it—the fact that I can't keep my hands off her.

Being good in bed is a gift. A woman shouldn't work at being good; it's not what she does that makes her good, even if she does it beautifully. It is that you know she is doing what she *wants* to do more than anything else. Her pleasure in doing it makes her good—not her doing it to give you pleasure. A woman should love to make love a lot, and should want to make love to me at that particular moment.

I know from my experience after all these years what a girl likes. It's not signs out of bed, but the actual practice: what works well, as it were. I like to know all the things a girl likes because I derive most of my pleasure from giving pleasure. A woman isn't less good if she asks for what she wants, but she needn't ask at all if she's with the right man. It obviously depends on the man, if he is not inclined to do the things she likes, or if he doesn't know women well. A lot of men never bother to quite understand a woman's sexual requirements, and you have to know them before you make love to a woman. You have to know women well and to care about them.

I am never really disappointed in bed because I never go to bed just for the sake of it. I don't mean that I have an emotional attachment or involvement with a girl before I go to bed with her, but that I am incapable of just making love without giving some feeling away—even if it is just for the moment. Therefore, I am never totally disappointed because I give something and I receive something in return. My personal taste is for giving pleasure to the woman, so if she doesn't have pleasure, then I have not had my own. But for a man who doesn't care, who takes his pleasure selfishly, it doesn't make any difference. If a man cares and a woman takes a long time to have an orgasm, it's hard work for him and can be very tiresome. I think, though, that women often fake. But it's not total fake—they get caught up when they fake, and the faking gives them some kind of pleasure, stimulates them.

I can't tell by just looking at a woman if she is going to be good in bed; one is often very surprised. I don't particularly like slim women too much myself, but it's true most of the time that thin women are often better in bed. They seem to have more sexual drive, they are most sexually sensitive, they get to a high point of vibration more quickly. You find, for instance, that girls with large nipples, bigger nipples, get much more excited more quickly and usually thin girls have bigger nipples.

Usually beauty doesn't make a woman good in bed—quite the opposite. Beautiful women make less effort in bed because since they were little everybody has said, "Look at that pretty girl," and it's enough. Usually when a girl is very pretty it is as if she makes you a present when she makes love to you: "Here I am—I am beautiful—everybody wants me—here, I give it to you—I'm doing you a big favor." Whereas a girl who is less pretty makes more effort; she says thank you all the time you are sleeping with her.

Experience makes a woman better in bed, but not experience for its own sake. What experience means, I think, is that a girl who is experienced is experienced because she likes making love and has done it. Therefore, if a girl has no experience, it means she hasn't had any particular drive to make love, she hasn't had a strong enough desire not to be able to resist the temptation.

Generally I would say that women over thirty are definitely much better in bed. It's because I think they are more free—they have got over all the inhibitions. When you are young—however free you are in your ideas and your life—you retain inhibitions for a certain time until you liberate yourself totally and get used to being totally naked without any feelings of discomfort or of doing anything wrong. Maybe women over thirty are so good because they have an inner compulsion to have sex as often as they can and get the best of it before they are no longer desirable.

The woman who is very cold-blooded about sex, who is there just to be slept with, is bad in bed. Usually if she has that attitude before bed, when you get to the time of making love she just gets down to the business of it—that's not so interesting. I wouldn't get any pleasure from doing anything that the woman didn't particularly like to do. And if she didn't particularly like to do the things that I did, that's what I would call being bad.

It's a question of having the same tastes, because people have tastes in bed the same way as they have tastes in food and drink, and you have to find the woman who has the same tastes as you have. So the woman who is good in bed has the same tastes as I have.

I have known girls of all nationalities, and my ideal woman in bed would be French. French girls are not pretty in my opinion—the standard of beauty in France is much lower than in England—but French girls do an enormous amount with what they've got. Whereas English girls lose a lot from when they wake up in the morning to when they go out—they don't know how to make the best of the beauty they do have. I live in France—and French girls are totally feminine. They have a way of cuddling a man's sexual parts—of really loving them. It's the real love for it. French girls are totally the woman, compared to, for example, the American woman, who's rather aggressive and dominating. The French woman never puts herself on the same level as the man sexually—a woman can't do that.

The man has got to feel some kind of domination, and the woman has to feel dominated in the act of love. A man (in terms of cliches) usually gets on top; it's not the best thing, but usually it's the attitude. He has to get the erection, and an erection is something powerful.Whereas the woman has a more passive role, she is the receptacle. The more a woman makes the man feel a man, the stronger his erection. If a woman dominates a man, even ever so slightly—or they are both on an equal level—then the man is emasculated.

Oriental woman are the opposite of aggressive in an exaggerated way. You come in and they will feed the man aphrodisiacs, they wash your parts, they perfume you, and you are sitting there with the feeling that you have a servant girl—a slave girl. You had slave girls in the past—all that was very exciting to men, slave girls, servant girls. Men like to go to prostitutes because they work for you, they work on you. A woman should retain some of that in her relationship with a man. There should be a combination of the man knowing the woman is *not* an inferior and that she is only *sexually* subservient, not in her everyday life; that she is playing the game, the role of being submissive during the act of love. A woman should know how to play a submissive role because the man wants to give to his woman, wants to protect her, wants to fuck her and give her pleasure, so she should make him feel strong by being extremely feminine. During the act of love it is important that the woman seems to be subservient, but only in these circumstances because the act of love is a relationship of dominating and being dominated.

Some women who are not *really* submissive love this attitude during the act of love. That is very good for them, and these women would be good. But submissive does not mean passive. Definitely not. Being submissive at the cost of their own pleasure is the worst thing—that's bad. In my opinion a woman should not do anything she does not like to do, not even to please the man. If he is pleased by things she doesn't like to do naturally, then they are not made for each other sexually. It can be good when it is acquired, but that is not as good as when it's good because it's natural. A woman should not try to be good; a woman is good when she is herself—if *herself* pleases the man she is with. And the man is good if he is himself—if *himself* pleases the woman he is with. You have to find the person who has the same sexual tastes; that is difficult, but when you do, you will be good in bed for each other.

JAMES CAAN

What makes a woman G.I.B.? Love.

STACY KEACH

Stacy Keach, the star of such movies as Conduct Unbecoming *and* Fat City, *and the TV series* Caribe, *has earned his reputation as a fine dramatic actor on the New York stage. Stacy and I had lunch with his secretary Debbie, and the interview ended up as a very animated discussion.*

One of the most exciting things about sex is that the woman who is good in bed is as variable as people themselves. You can look at a woman who is absolutely gorgeous, and then find out that she is boring in bed, and you can look at another woman who is not so beautiful, but if you go to bed with her, you might be surprised. All of my feelings about a woman have to do with states of being: perceptiveness, openness, willingness, tenderness.

The trouble is that some people have problems about sexual relationships because they have subjective expectations rather than allowing an experience to happen. Expectations start with Mother and Dad and friends and society. In America, sexuality in the past twenty years has undergone a tremendous change, and the whole Victorian sexual ethic has been shattered. The free love era of the sixties made people suddenly realize that it was all right to feel, touch, and explore one another's physicality, without necessarily having any emotional attachment beyond the experience itself.

I still am chauvinistic in my attitudes. I came to enjoy, in my teens, the whole aspect of opening car doors and picking up checks and being chivalrous, but when the new ethic struck all of our consciousnesses, I found myself put down for being condescending and patronizing. It was all very disturbing for me, so my reaction became very defensive.

However things have changed, lack of involvement still makes a woman bad in bed; also resistance to explore—to allow herself to be open. Personally, I think a woman is less good in bed if she refuses a specific demand I make. There is a spirit involved in sexual activity which is not just simply a casual need to satisfy physical desires; it's a willingness to engage in sexual play together and to please one another sexually. Resistance is totally antithetical to the whole concept of pleasure.

But refusal prior to bed is exciting for a man. Anticipation is often better than the reality of an experience. I am talking about the woman who is attracted to a man, but who says, "Oh, we don't know each other well enough," or, "It's the wrong time," or "I'd love to, but I have to get home to my husband." If the desire has already been established and then resistance follows, I feel *that* heightens the excitement of the ultimate encounter.

Of course there has to *be* an ultimate encounter, because men feel blind loathing and hatred for women who come on strong and then say, "Bye-bye." That's a sort of manipulative technique which very young girls often adopt. I really mean coyness—a very feminine quality, a very sexual quality, and a manifestation of sexual desire. It reflects willingness without the directness of "Let's fuck," and is somehow more civilized and more ladylike. The best example of coyness in terms of art is found in Restoration comedy. There the degree of the coyness is in direct proportion to the degree of the desire; the game is to let this unravel slowly. It is a form of loveplay or foreplay; the pushing of someone away with one hand, and the pulling them toward you with the other.

My wife is the first woman who ever propositioned me. I met her at a beach house; we were walking along the beach when suddenly she said, "I would love to go to bed with you." At the time, I was involved with another lady, but this approach excited me tremendously, so we made an appointment to see each other that evening. I showed up but she didn't. Later she admitted that she stood me up because of being nervous. I was livid—as I was all excited. I didn't see her again for four years, but we kept up a correspondence and finally ended up getting married.

I once had an experience where I met a woman and there was immediate attraction, so five or six hours later, we were in bed together. I remember between the fifth and sixth hour before we finally hit the sack I experienced so many different kinds of emotion: "This is much too easy; there's not enough build-up." Then there was the other side—the excitement of saying, "Isn't this nice?" It was so simple, but there was still the telltale feeling that it was *too* convenient and comfortable. The whole situation worked out on the positive side, because the *desire* and the *passion* were the turn-on.

The first time in bed with any woman is still an adventure—a new terrain, a new experience. So the first time is usually good with every woman, no matter who she is. I love hookers, myself. They are what they are—with no emotional complications. They provide an experience of sexual gratification with no emotional pretense—pure and simple. A hooker is good in bed if she goes beyond the price and time and makes that extra little effort if she likes you.

Love adds something to bed, but I am not sure what. I don't really, I guess, in my heart of hearts, believe that love and sex are interconnected in the way that religion has made it appear. I am not sure I make that equation. When you love somebody, the feeling of love doesn't always have sexual connotations because it transcends sex—is beyond it. I believe that the feeling of love does not require the sexual act to sustain it, and I think that the reverse must therefore apply: that sex does not require love to sustain it.

But love can ruin sex, because if you don't feel like having sex with your mate, you may meet a reaction like, "You don't love me if you don't want to fuck me." And that's not true. "I love you, but I just want to go to sleep." If you are tired, have been working all day, and the woman is taking a long time to come, she sometimes *does* seem less good.

Really, sex is something that brings people together. You can have a non-sexual relationship with somebody, write a script together, take a trip together, and the degree to which that event was good or bad involves the same things: rapport, togetherness, willingness to listen, and to respond to the other person—to give and to take.

RYAN O'NEAL

What makes a woman G.I.B? My father used to say, "It's either good or better."

MARJORIE WALLACE

Marjorie Wallace and I spent hours over tea and lunch talking about the horrors of Hollywood—about insistent film producers and agents determined to bed us. I had been in London in 1973 when Marjorie won and lost the Miss World title, and I was surprised to discover that she was only nineteen when her name hit the headlines. Marjorie has obviously thought very seriously about all the publicity and the problems caused by her Miss World victory. Marjorie Wallace really is one of the world's most beautiful women, but far from being unapproachable, she actually wrote her own piece for this book.

Miss World didn't really change me. My basic attitudes toward myself, life, sex, and men have always been the same: I don't go to bed with somebody I don't like a lot. I don't expect him to put me on a pedestal and say that I am the greatest and the best; it would probably be bullshit, anyway.

I usually start with a man on a mutual respect basis, so whether the sex is astronomical, just all right, or just plain bad, if I really like the guy I give it a chance. Sometimes it turns out really great; and if there is no next time, then it is still all right. So I've never worried about whether it's right or wrong or what he'll think, because most of all I try to be true to myself. And, as we all know, you come this way but once (through this life, I mean).

I don't think that becoming Miss World made me more

confident in myself as a woman. Actually I lost a lot of self-assurance. I went from a stage of knowing myself, being myself, and being with friends who accepted me for what I was. Then all of a sudden—boom—there I was in the public eye, suddenly at everybody else's liberty to discuss me, look at me, evaluate me, build me up, tear me down. Instant insecurity: when you walk into a room and there are people nudging each other and saying, "There she is, there she is. She is pretty; she should have won," or, "She is not pretty; she should never have won. She's probably a bitch." But then I realized that I am me, and if I stay me then I will survive. Maybe!

Every day men wanted to make it with me; I was flattered at first; then skepticism and paranoia set in. But when you spend time with someone, you get looser and looser. Now I am not afraid to ask for what I want in bed, because I am a human being and I know that the person lying next to me is one too and that we all have our thoughts, our "maybes," and our "I wonder ifs," and so that makes us even. I know that for everything I might ask him and might wonder about and need, I know that he is lying there having some of the same thoughts going through his heart and mind. So you should always remember that it is not just you, it is the rest of the world, too, so we are all even.

If you can look at each other and just realize your equality, you have a healthy thing going for you. I think that if you are in love with the man, you can be fantastic, but not really be any different than you were with another man a week ago whom you were not in love with. You can do the same things the same way, but unless you have that emotional involvement, the whole thing's a different story.

Also, a man has a lot to do with it by the way he treats a woman. I am not an extremely calculating person; I love life and I love love, and if somebody wants to share that with me, it's fine. But I don't plan a week or a year ahead. I am here and if we are smiling, we are smiling, and if we are not, then we will deal with that.

If a virgin asked my advice on how to be good in bed, I would say, "Just believe in yourself, and know that you are strong, you are capable of doing it, and if you don't want to, then you should be capable of saying no. If you are strong within yourself, and if you believe in your own convictions and are satisfied with yourself, you will then be able to satisfy the man beside you."

DEBBIE REYNOLDS

What makes a woman G.I.B? I am not exactly the sexy one to ask, I suppose. I think first of all to go to bed to sleep, you should exercise a great deal. To go to bed to be a great love mate, you have to love the man a great deal.

ALAN KING

I met comedian and show business impresario Alan King in Las Vegas during the Alan King Tennis Tournament.

Appreciation and warmth make a woman good in bed. In the past, I have found that the women who look as if they might be the best in bed are usually the most disappointing. I believe sensuality isn't something as obvious as just a physical look. I think that Sophia Loren would be the ideal woman to have in bed; of course, I have never met her, but she is very earthy, very voluptuous, a good, strong face, has great character, and seems very exciting, judging from what I have read and heard about her. I think she is my fantasy woman.

I don't think a woman is less good if she asks for what she wants in bed. I'm always happy to accommodate. If she refuses anything in bed? Well, that's a very bad time to start an argument. I don't know very many women who are bad in bed. I find, generally speaking, that if you have got to the point of being in bed with a woman, it has usually been very pleasant getting there in the first place, so it usually ends up being very nice.

SONNY BONO

What makes a woman G.I.B? Good bloodline, background, and breeding.

MARTY FELDMAN

Successful comedy transplant from England, Marty Feldman shot immediately to the top in America through his work with Mel Brooks and Gene Wilder in such movies as Sherlock Holmes' Smarter Brother, Young Frankenstein, *and* Silent Movie. *He did this interview at Universal Studios, while he was scripting* The Last Remake of Beau Geste, *which he will star in and direct.*

I think we are given false expectations about sex, so it never quite measures up to the way sex is in the movies. Sex is the satisfaction of an appetite. It *can* be more than that, but it usually is far less than the media portrays. People get a lot of their ideas about sex from media exaggerations, so now both men and women have some abstract idea of the proper sexual relationship. It's a kind of sexual nirvana which I don't think many people experience.

I found my first sexual experience terribly dissatisfying because I expected it to be cosmic; it was merely enjoyable in the same way as when I first ate houmous. I had heard about it for years, and I happened to like it, but it didn't wake my tastebuds up—I didn't leap around—it was very pleasurable.

If I were looking for the perfect woman in bed, I would look for one who tries to please me. Someone who is flexible and will experiment on an equal basis. That seems to me a reasonable basis for any relationship, be it sexual or professional, or professionally sexual or sexually professional—whichever way you come at it, or go at it.

Sex is a collaboration in the truest sense; you both work together for a common end. After all, my life started with a collaboration between my father and my mother (at least I assume it was my father; I have no proof). Collaboration runs through life, and the more you do something together—the more you understand each other's responses and needs—the more you become a team. Sex is not very different from a soccer team—the end is different, but the means are the same. Teamwork is understanding each other's needs and the cause and effect; the effect will be mutual, the causes will be different.

I knew I could act with Gene Wilder the minute we met. Chemistry. Had Gene Wilder been an attractive woman, it would have been a sexual vibration. I can't define it. If you could define what makes a woman or a man good in bed, then everybody would do it well, and there would be no mystery in bed.

If two people are inexperienced, they will learn together; if one person is experienced, he will teach the other; if they're both very experienced, then they will both get much more fulfillment and enjoyment out of sex. If you get two skillful performers at it, they will know how to collaborate. Love can matter in bed, but I know people who believe they're in love with everyone they sleep with; perhaps they *are* just for that time.

Sex needn't always be equal, but if not, it is by choice. There are times when you don't feel like making the going and the woman makes the going. And there are other times when the man makes the approach, controls the act, the tempo. The approach doesn't make any difference, as long as both people are getting maximum enjoyment out of sex, but you decide everything for yourself. You don't let anyone else decide for you.

People *do* try and decide what is sexually normal and what is a deviation. I hate to hear the word "deviation" because I have yet to see "the norm" defined. When I see it defined, then I can discuss what is abnormal. I don't know what is normal. None of us do, because we don't live in each other's bedrooms. Normal is whatever you enjoy. To quote Hemingway: "What is moral is what you feel good after." Any relationship with a predator or a prey is not equal and is therefore nor moral or normal.

Sex is two plus two making five, rather than four. Sex is the X ingredient that you can't define, and it's that X ingredient between two people that makes both a man and a woman good in bed. It's all relative. There are no rules. But if there *were* a rule for good sex, it would be: "Play it by ear," except, I suppose, the ear is the wrong organ.

PETER USTINOV

What makes a woman G.I.B? Sex is conversation carried out by other means. If you get on well out of bed, half the problems of bed are solved. Sex is good if you understand someone—not if you are just attracted to her physically and nothing else. I can't take a flip attitude to this subject—it's very serious.

ZSA ZSA GABOR

I waited six hours for Zsa Zsa Gabor at the Connaught Hotel in London, but the final interview was worth waiting for. That original interview was not for this book, but indirectly led to it, because afterwards, Zsa Zsa suggested to me that I should come to Hollywood. I did, and we met again for tea, then lunch, at her house in Bel Air, and talked for hours. She showed me the house and her dressing room, which is like a department store, with all the clothes covered in plastic, catalogued, and hanging in rows. Zsa Zsa went straight to one of those rows, took out an orange and amber chiffon nightgown and said: "Darling, this is for you—it matches your hair perfectly." It did.

I hate anything learned about sex—anything that is not instinctive. Studied sex is terrible. I hate it. My last husband was like that. He studied everything about sex. He went to classes to learn how to make love. I personally think that when two people like each other, then sex comes naturally. But if they don't like each other, then neither of them will be good in bed.

A woman is born sexy. She can't learn to be sexy. I think

you're either sexy or you're not, and a really sexy man can recognize a really sexy woman. You can't become sexy, but surely a man whom you love can make you more sexy if you are not. I would never give advice on being good in bed. If anyone wants advice on that, they should go to a professional woman for it. I never ever have to think about being sexy, because I only go to bed with a person I want to go to bed with and whom I like, so of course that will be good. I think that the man is the most important performer in bed—he has to have the upper hand. I am very feminine—I like the man to take over. Then I react.

I only go to bed with a man I'm very attracted to, have a crush on, or I am madly in love with. Sometimes you can find out immediately if you are attracted to a man—sometimes it develops. Some women are much more receptive to men than others because they are born to like men—they are not just sexy, they like being with men. But then there are some women who don't really like men. I am not talking about lesbians. I am talking about women who don't like men as sexual beings.

I don't believe in good or bad in bed. I believe if a woman is in love and sexy, she will be fantastic in bed. A sexy woman is a woman who likes to make love. It has nothing to do with looks. I think you have to please the man first and then automatically you please yourself. I don't think you need to be in love to be good, you have to have a very strong attraction to someone, and if there is that sexual attraction you'll both be good, but a great sexual attraction doesn't happen often between people. I have always attracted men naturally. I never make any special efforts. I like men and I like to sleep with men that I like. Obviously, I am not a cold woman; a man likes a woman who is not cold, and I think that they recognize that in me.

When you are in bed with a man you love or are attracted to, you don't have to talk about what you like—everything comes naturally. The best way to lose a man is to not let him be his natural self. I think in bed the woman has to be natural, and has to really want to be with the man she is in bed with. Then everything comes naturally. But you really have to be in ecstasy, and when a woman is in ecstasy, she can do anything she wants. Ecstasy has not been rare in my life, but when the ecstasy is gone, I am gone, too. I never stay longer than the ecstasy.

I also think there should be some jealousy in a relationship, because when jealousy is gone, it becomes a boring, dreary relationship. It is good to understand a man, but you don't want to know everything about him. You want to be a little puzzled about what he is going to do next.

I never faked anything in my life, but if a woman is definitely subdued with a man, he will like it. A tough and bossy woman is only good for a weak man who wants a tough and bossy woman. I always liked men who are stronger than I am, and the moment I encounter a weak man, I scare him to death and he runs from me anyhow. Building up a man's ego makes *him* better in bed. He will also be more appreciative of a woman. A man who is not Mr. Big has to be built up. He becomes better in bed when he is made to feel like Mr. Big.

Men who really *are* Mr. Big don't need that so much—they want honesty. If a man is very successful and intelligent, then that kind of man always wants an honest woman, and of course a woman who turns him on. But however honest one tries to be with Mr. Big, a woman still has to subdue herself even for a man like that. The big catches all married little subdued women. Those kinds of women built a man up so he felt more masculine.

A very successful and famous man, if he is not spoiled, is a wonderful pleasure to be with, but if he is spoiled, the relationship won't last, because then he is much too big a chore for a woman. It's also very difficult for two famous people to have a man-woman relationship. If the woman is as successful as the man, then she always has to underplay her success so that the man will always feel superior. To be the wife or girlfriend of a successful man is also very difficult because every other woman in the world is after him. Famous male sex symbols, for example, have some special kind of attraction for women which turns them on—a kind of magnetism. It doesn't mean, though, that everyone of those magnetic, charismatic, exciting, masculine-looking male stars are really sexy. Usually they are not.

If a woman wants special-status men, she has to be special, and that's very difficult. One man wants a very simple, nice woman; the other wants a very difficult and mysterious woman—so you have to find out what that particular man wants, and then you have to live up to it.

You have to try and change yourself for every man you're with. I never did, but a woman should try. You should try to be like the man wants you to be, but that doesn't mean you have to lose your personality, because if you do that, if you lose your personality, you lose what the man fell in love with in the first place. He fell in love with you as you are, so obviously that is what he wants.

I was always honest with men, but you shouldn't always let a man know how much you care about him. He should never be 100 percent sure that you belong to him, and he should always doubt that you love him. Many men get turned off when you tell them how much you care about them. It's a bore not to be able to tell a man how you feel about him, because if you really love him, it's wonderful to tell him so. You can only tell a really mature, intelligent man exactly how you feel about him.

I think a man likes to chase a woman. The big fault of the American woman is that she chases a man. I think that's very bad. I think I kept Rubirosa so much in love with me always when all the women in the world wanted him because I never really was in love with him. I was in love with George Sanders (who was my husband), but Rubirosa was so exciting, I couldn't resist him sexually. There was a terrific sexual attraction between us, and also he was one of the sweetest, dearest persons ever born. I think if I had been like all the other women in Rubirosa's life, madly in love with him, just making an enormous fuss of him and not letting him chase me, I would have lost him. But like this I never lost Rubirosa—he was always in love with me, was never sure of me, and that was right.

George Sanders did the same to me, and I always loved him. I loved George for the simple reason that he knew how much I needed and loved him. George was so difficult and so interesting; he was such an exciting man, so he always had me dangling off his little finger. He was a challenge because he was intelligent, sophisticated, and very aloof, and that excited me so much. Challenges *are* exciting, but you can never feel comfortable with a man you can never really capture. It is good to be with a man who loves you and looks after you and really cares about you, but that is *not* usually the man who doesn't want you—whom you want—who challenges you. And I have found out since that a woman has to have other challenges in life—not just a man.

GEORGE SEGAL

What makes a woman G.I.B? A man makes a woman good in bed—the one who is right.

ELLIOTT GOULD

Elliott Gould was everywhere I went in Beverly Hills—every reception, every party, on Sunset Boulevard, at the Beverly Hills Hotel—not intentionally, but just because he is one of the most accessible celebrities I know. But I was a bit apprehensive before the interview; a journalist I knew had just been reduced to tears because Elliott and James Caan had clowned all the way throughout an interview she had tried to keep serious. But, when I went to his house in Beverly Hills, Elliott, dressed in dungarees, discussed the subject very seriously.

What makes a woman good in bed? It's great to talk about this. I like to be handled gently. Being a large individual, I like to be handled as gently as I am expected to handle my mate. You should be able to tell if a woman is good. She has to have clear eyes and two ears. There is no physical type. Experience makes a woman. A woman of experience, just like a man of experience, would be able to listen, and able to direct in bed.

It's great if a woman asks for what she wants in bed. I love a woman who is point blank, is specific. If a woman can ask, say, "This is what I want" (we try not to want anything—not to need anything and just to be, just to exist) and can be direct and tell you what it is that is necessary for her to begin, or end, that's great. A woman is not less good if she refuses something. Sometimes it is even more enticing if she refuses to go along.

Women worry about being good in bed, and so do men. Not to be understood. If you are misunderstood, you have failed in bed. I really don't see how a woman can be bad in bed if she shows up, but I suppose rigidity *is* bad in bed. The only thing that is *really* bad in bed is illness and sickness—also people thinking that bed is where sex is meant to be, that a bed should be a bedroom, because a bed can also be grass under a tree, on the beach. Basically, the only reason for being in a bed is to sleep.

They made *Great Expectations* but we, here, have no expectations and we say, "Don't expect anything other than being together," and then, wherever it takes you. One important thing is to be understood and to be touched. To be touched so that the two individuals always have their space and know where they begin and where they become part of each other.

Sex is different every time. Sex is different every time for the same two people—people who have a relationship and just want to spend time with one another. Sex should be new every time for the relationship to develop. I feel double values don't work in sex, and that two people have to be able to be one another, which is very stimulating—to be with someone I like, who can be me, and who I can be.

BRUCE DERN

What makes a woman G.I.B? Personally, I like a woman to be a whore in bed.

MARILYN CHAMBERS

The first time I met Marilyn Chambers was when she invited me to her birthday party. She burst into tears as the guests sang "Happy Birthday," and she was a million times removed from being the porno queen of Behind the Green Door. *We did three separate interviews for the book: one in Las Vegas, while she was appearing in* Mind with the Dirty Man; *one in New York, between rehearsals for* Le Bellybutton; *and one at the Algonquin Hotel in New York, where we had drinks and whispered about vibrators in an atmosphere of hushed respectability.*

Even though I know I am good in bed, I wasn't always good. I learned to be good, and I didn't always have orgasms. Some women haven't heard of self-manipulation. I hadn't. Then I discovered that I had to help myself come with self-manipulation. Then I masturbated with a vibrator, but always alone. So when I finally did it in front of a man, it was very interesting—he was very masculine, otherwise I would have been afraid to masturbate in front of him.

Some women are afraid to manipulate themselves when they are in bed with a man. I would masturbate in front of any man, because a lot of them don't understand that the inside of the vagina has no nerve endings. I have my best orgasms with finger manipulation. I control it. Most men are bad at manipulating a woman, so I prefer to do it to myself. If the man doesn't like me masturbating—that's too bad. I think a man should say, "Get your vibrator out," instead of you saying, "Can I use it?" It's a drag if you have to ask a man, and it makes you feel as if *you* are less good.

I'm sure I've been in situations where a man has made me feel bad in bed. Then I get an unacceptable feeling that makes me not want to be with him anyway. Sometimes it's important, for example, for people to make noises and then lose control. But if you have to restrain yourself, you never lose control.

I've had a man tell me to be quiet in bed, and that's terrible. Why should you be, when the whole point of having an orgasm is to lose control? I've had one man say, "Why are you so loud? Why do you make so much noise?"

A woman can be good in bed and still not have an orgasm,

but I always have one, sometimes three or four, depending on how tired or how turned-on I am. I think it is always up to the woman to have her orgasm.

I need vibrators and dildos just to get myself loosened up, but I prefer my finger, because it doesn't make any noise. I think vibrator noise is a real turn-off. It kills fantasies and you can't concentrate. When you start using a vibrator, you can keep coming on and on all day. What's really good is a hose in your bathtub. You just die—I swear. You really do. You just hook a hose to the faucet, and take the spray attachment off; then it's just a hose. The water pressure gets you off, and you have the most wrenching orgasms you will ever have in your life. You put it on your clit, then you turn the water up and down—hot or cold—and you go through the ceiling.

I have never refused anything in bed. Of course I was afraid of giving head at first, of the unknown. One time I had a really weird experience. I really dug this guy. I was giving him head, and he suddenly got freaked out, pushed me away, and said I bit him. He didn't seem to want me to give him head. (Sometimes I do like to use my teeth—but no biting, just slightly.) This was when I was very inexperienced. I didn't have any idea how to give head or "deep throat," but still I didn't bite this guy.

Later I found out that once he had been asleep and he suddenly woke up to find his stepfather giving him head. He was really sexually screwed up because of that, and really had a sexual problem about head; that's why he said I bit him. I felt really bad, and that it was my fault. But then I realized that however good I really was, there was nothing I could do about his problem because it *wasn't* my fault.

Giving head is important. Giving head to an uncircumcised man is a totally different trip from a circumcised man. When a prick is circumcised, it doesn't matter how much you go down and up. But if you push the skin down on uncircumcised pricks, it's uncomfortable for the man. Uncircumcised pricks are very sensitive, so you have to open your mouth as you go down the shaft and close it when you come up; you can't shut your mouth and go down; you musn't push the skin down. It's a whole learning thing. I had to be taught by the man, and you need a patient man.

Giving good head makes a woman good in bed. I also like getting fucked in the throat—deep throat—relaxing my muscles; opening your throat is the main thing. I had good compliments when I started out and now I know how to do it better. It's not just relaxing the muscles and knowing how to give deep throat, it's also loving pricks. I love pricks; no matter how big or small, I always get horny.

I am better in bed with men now that I have been with a woman. I know what I like. I know what another woman wants, and I know what turns me on. Now I also know that the taste of pussy is not obnoxious. I have had men act as if giving me head was a great favor. A lot of men don't like to eat pussy because they think it's dirty. Occasionally, men have made me aware they felt like that. I know I am always clean, but if a guy doesn't want to give head, I don't think less of him. If he doesn't eat me automatically, I never ask him to. I am able to say, "Well, if you don't, that's cool." I don't want to have to force the subject. If *he* doesn't want to, I would still give him head, because I like to give and to please—I get pleasure from giving pleasure.

I think I'm good with every single man I've had sex with. Once I had sex blindfolded. I had about seven men. I had no choice. It was a bondage situation, and I had no say. It was lovely—totally submissive. A lot of women don't admit that they would like to be raped. Rape, though, is a bad word. I don't mean real rape, being brutally beaten up, but being taken against your will, like in a fantasy, with pain turning into pleasure. Before Chuck, I didn't ask other men to act out any of my submissive fantasies. I didn't know what I really wanted. But I also thought, "If I ask for that, I might turn him off." I didn't know whether what I wanted was normal. Then, what is normal? I know I am normal.

If a woman asked me for advice on how to be good, I would tell her to learn how to relax. That is the most important thing. It's sort of self-hypnosis, so the mind tells you to relax. I believe your mind controls your body totally, and unless your mind is into sex, your body won't be; then, if you don't know how to let yourself go, you'll never have an orgasm. Relax, then turn the guy on. Go down on him. Then he will know you want to turn him on.

I do a lot to be good in bed, and I know men can *tell* I'm good because I look innocent. So they think they can take advantage of me. I know how to turn myself on to turn a man on, and a man isn't turned on unless a woman is. I do a lot of exercises, I dance to music. I do Kegel exercises as often as I can to tighten the vagina. You tighten your muscles, you tighten your rear end, your legs, and sort of close your vagina. It's like tightening your stomach.

Fantasies matter, and women should tell a man their sexual fantasies. When the sex has become boring, you want to liven it up, meet him at the door in black boots and a whip if he is into S/M. Or meet him with nothing on, just an apron and a drink. Do little things to please your lover all the time. If a guy likes to tie you up, have all the rope right there and say, "Hey, let's do this" so he doesn't have to suggest it.

I don't make love to just anyone I meet, only very special people. I went to bed with Xaviera Hollander. What makes her good? She is dominant, and she knows what she is doing. She knows how to please herself. She has had a lot of experience, and experience is the most important thing which makes a woman good in bed. You can't help but get better with experience. Xaviera has been with all different types of men and women in all different situations. She knows how to start a fantasy. You wouldn't have to suggest a scene—she would just know what you wanted by meeting you.

I like masochistic fantasies. I always like a man who is rough with me. I am basically always the same in bed, although obviously with even more experience I might change my attitudes. I have become more submissive because I have learned that I am basically a masochist. But again, perhaps one day I might change and become a sadist.

Being good in bed is doing everything the man wants. You must never refuse anything, because refusing will make you into an individual. You can't be an individual and be good in bed as well.

RICHARD BURTON

What makes a woman G.I.B? Glamor and beauty have got nothing to do with what makes a woman good in bed. A woman is good if you can talk to her, but more important, if you can laugh with her afterwards.

GLENDA JACKSON

Glenda Jackson did this interview in her dressing room at the Old Vic in London while she was putting her hair into curlers before a performance of The White Devil. *She had obviously considered the subject carefully, and was incredibly articulate, yet she never once faltered with a single curler.*

I have always resented the phrase "good in bed." I have heard men use it—although I must admit that I have never considered it in relation to myself. I take umbrage at it because the concept is part of the myth of a woman being evaluated as a human being only on a very specific level, in a very limited area—with the judge, jury, and hangman in that particular assessment being a man.

It is always very difficult to know what men mean when they say a woman is good in bed. I think that a man thinks a woman is good if she tells him *he* is. So, more often than not, "good" to men, I think, means that the woman has said or done something that has flattered their ego. Some men have a fantasy that they are wondrous in bed, and if they feel they are not, they will turn around and say, "It is your fault." But men worry much more about their reputations with one another than with women. So I think that the phrase "good in bed" is a generality that men make for each other when they boast about their sexual exploits.

Any assessment of good seems to be grossly unfair. It is unwritten that it is possible to be bad in bed if you say someone is good. It also infers that there is something durable and positive in someone who is good—and something diminishing and demeaning in somebody who is bad. But I don't think that is the case or that the judgment should be made at all. People are not born bad or good in bed. Personally speaking, I think sex is terrific—but there are people one knows who don't think it is. That is a programmed response, though, something that has happened to them, part of their upbringing and nothing to do with being born good or bad.

When I was at school there seemed to be very little fantasy of the actual sex act or process, because sex was still strictly on the level of how boys looked, of what made them attractive. We were told that to participate was sufficient—to enjoy sex was not necessary. In any case, then the great danger was not whether you were good or whether you were bad; it was whether you got pregnant. We didn't consider being good; there was a certain belief that you would automatically know what to do, and if you didn't, the man would. I don't think it ever occurred to us to wonder what *we* had to do.

I think today we worry far too much. It's part of our particular society at the moment that people think sex is desperately important and are particularly vulnerable about it and about their own abilities in that particular area. I think sex is terribly funny if you think about it. If it is taken as a life-and-death situation, then it will be a total disaster. And even then, if it is lousy, then it's lousy and there are reasons other than physical dexterity or imaginativeness or reading the *Kama Sutra*.

You don't buy being good in bed off a shelf. I don't think there is a program you go through with someone which results in what you expected when you first put your penny in the slot. I don't think it's anything that exists outside your whole self; it is not an area you can put on and take off. It is as much part of what you are as a person—like your predilection in food or holidays, clothes or literature. It is an intrinsic part of you and I don't think you can adopt other people's attitudes and practices.

Whether you are good in bed or not can only be evaluated in a moment: how much you experience, how much the other person experiences. And that is not a moment clouded in mystery. You either know or you don't know; it's either working for you or it isn't. But I don't think sex works all the time, and even with people with whom it works for *you* all the time; there are ups and downs within that situation. If you are in a continuing relationship and the sex isn't working over a long period of time, then the two people should work it out together.

I think you can have a good sexual relationship with a total stranger. It has never really happened to me, but I can see no reason why it shouldn't. Just simply a straight physical turn-on by someone you haven't met before. It would probably work if it didn't conflict too strongly with your view of yourself, of your own particular moral strictures. But it's very difficult to separate sex and morality (even though I think they should be separated). In any case, if there is a temporary relationship and the sex doesn't work, each person can go their separate way, equally free to accuse the other person of being bad in bed. Except that that judgment should only be made to someone on the clear understanding that the judgment is based on only *one* experience.

My experience of men is very limited because I was married for a very, very long time. When you go virtually from school to being married, your experience of sex is so totally limited, even to the level of what you like. That is something you will hopefully learn with someone who will teach you well, and I think I was probably very fortunate. If anyone asked me the way to be good in bed, I would tell them, preferably being in bed with a fellow you wanted to be with and who wanted to be with you.

I think it would be quite difficult for the woman to be good for the man, yet not enjoy sex herself. If that does happen in a very honest relationship, I think the woman has a responsibility to say, "Look, without wishing to be critical or totally destroy you, you may think that I am having the most wonderful time in the world, but a time arrives when it all stops for me." That has to be said, otherwise resentment will build up and the relationship will then be destroyed. I would say that to someone, but it is difficult, because men are very sensitive in that area. They are often taught that men are automatically good in bed, and so they sometimes lack the urge to admit that they are *not* automatically so. Therefore, their whole ethos is to preserve that fantasy for themselves, which makes it very difficult for a woman to admit a lack of actual sexual satisfaction.

I think women can be infinitely kinder, gentler, more loving, and more hopeful. They always believe in tomorrow; they don't stay with the situation they are in; they always believe that there will be something better; they are essentially optimistic. Because of that, a woman would probably put up with a relationship that she did not regard as good on a sexual level, that did not give her sexual satisfaction. I am not sure that the same is true of men.

Men do sometimes try to exert pressure to get what they want in bed. I have never been in an actual situation where a man has made me feel sexually inadequate because I didn't do something that he has wanted—where he has tried to exert any pressure on me. In other areas men have tried—like using the old trick, when I am winning an argument,of saying, "Well, you're too intelligent to be feminine." I have had that a lot. And always, in all situations, my intelligence has told me the truth of those situations, the facts, whereas my emotions probably pulled me another way. That is a split I have always had and always will have, but I think it depends on your mood as to which you actually observe.

I think men also try to exert sexual pressure by saying, "If you love me, you would do it." If that happened, I would say, "If you can say that to me, you don't actually love me, so what the fuck am I doing with you anyway?" Then the relationship would be over. If I didn't want to do something sexually, there would be no pressure on earth the man could exert that would make me do it, and I wouldn't give a fuck how much the man said, "You're no good." In any case, I don't believe that there's a general definition of "good in bed" to be made. It is just something that has to be defined by each person for themselves.

JAMES DARREN

What makes a woman G.I.B? A woman is good if she doesn't spit the apple seeds in your face afterwards.

Part III

The Glamor Professionals

GEORGE BEST

Soccer Star

George Best, English soccer star, was the first player sold on the strength of his sex appeal as well as his universally acclaimed skill. At the time of this interview he was playing for the Los Angeles Aztecs, was living peacefully in a beach house, and did this entire interview dressed in a beach towel.

Fifty percent of the time I am with a woman who is good in bed. Being a professional sportsman, I get groupies like entertainers do, but eventually I get fed up. I have now got to the stage where I'd rather spend time in bed with a girl who has a bit more intelligence—not just looks. Looks aren't that important to me now. They were when I was younger and liked to be seen with a beautiful woman. But now, that is not that important to me. Looks don't show whether a girl is good in bed or not. I know you've got to get into bed with a girl before you can find out if she is good because I have looked at girls and thought they would be good, but have been disappointed, and vice versa.

So I don't believe there are any visible signs out of bed that the woman is either good or bad. You just have to go on and do it. Usually, though, the exhibitionistic type of girl is not very good in bed, and the quieter type is better. So in a club or a bar I am always more attracted to the girl who just sits there. I suppose it's just ego, because the girl sitting there not smiling presents a challenge. It may be harder to attract her. In Los Angeles, things are different. As no one knows me here, it's lovely—I have to do everything on my own merits, whereas in England, it was easy to find girls.

If I were Frankenstein, able to create the ideal woman in bed, or if I could pick any woman in the world to go to bed with, I would want Sarah Miles. Judging by what I've seen and read of her, I think she's a beautiful woman—very talented, and also very intelligent. What more do you want? But, then again, I change. Next month it might be someone else. Otherwise I would like a gymnast; the outdoor athletic type appeals to most men, I think. There is something really beautiful about a woman with an unbelievable shape, who is fit, fresh, healthy, and looks good. I like an outdoor type of girl: blonde hair with natural looks, like the beach girls you get down here in Redondo Beach where I live.

I had the choice of staying anywhere in Los Angeles and picked Redondo Beach. Originally I was going to stay in Beverly Hills, but I think that in the last couple of years, I myself have changed, and I would much rather be down here at the beach, where it's not as false. If I want to spend a couple of days in Beverly Hills, I can, but I couldn't live in a place like that. I find it false. Actresses and models—I can't stand the crap they come out with: "Where were you born?" and, "What is your birth sign?" It's all such a load of shit. It really turns me off.

I also get turned off if a woman needs a drink *before* she

goes to bed. That kind of woman is bad in bed. So is the woman who says, "I've got to have a smoke first." It implies that she can't do without help from outside sources, and that turns me off completely. Some women have got to a stage of thinking they need it, and I don't agree with that. If a man is good enough, and the woman wants to be with him enough, then she shouldn't need any stimulation. I don't smoke marijuana at all. It doesn't interest me. I've never tried it, and I never want to try it. Maybe I am an outsider looking in. I know you shouldn't knock something without trying it, but I do knock it, and that is a big thing I've got against some women—if they can't go to bed without smoking.

Good sex has definitely to do with the atmosphere between you. If a man feels it's too much of an effort to make a woman come, that's laziness. If the evening or the time is right, then it will never take a woman long to come. But if she does take a long time, it doesn't really matter.

As far as I am concerned, head is not that important. It is *not* vital. I think head is more sexy than actually being good in bed. There's a hell of a difference between being good in bed and being able to give head properly. A woman can be good at giving head in a car, or anywhere else, but not be good in bed.

A woman has to use her best attributes. I think the nicest thing is a woman who knows the sort of mood you're in, instinctively. It's nice on some nights, when I've been playing a game which hasn't gone well for me, to come home to a woman, have a couple of glasses of wine, and go to bed. Then, on nights like that, I don't want to have sex. I think a woman who is good realizes that and isn't selfish because she knows you can make up for it other nights.

Everybody has off days—men as well as women. I have refused things in bed and so have women I've been with. But if a woman doesn't feel like doing something I want in bed, I try very hard to change her mind. If she *still* doesn't feel like it, I just go to sleep.

JOHN O'GRADY

Private Detective

John O'Grady is Hollywood's number one private eye. An ex-detective sergeant from the Los Angeles police department, he has worked for Zsa Zsa Gabor, Andy Williams, Jane Russell, Peggy Lee, and Elvis Presley. O'Grady could double for Robert Mitchum.

The average woman isn't worth anything in bed. After thirty-five, women are ashamed to take their clothes off in front of a man. The plumbing has gone, they become very inhibited and have become Florence Nightingale—a mother. Women disappear at thirty. The blossom fades fast.

I don't think most women care about sex. It is a convenience for men; women have a different emphasis. I know five girls in their thirties—I have never been involved with them. They all have children, are well-built and good looking—all searching for a man. They all say that what they want is a man of thirty-five who will love their children. They never say that they are looking for a guy to ball the ass off them. Most women are lazy prostitutes. They think if they wriggle a little bit, that will be enough in bed, but they should really perform and satisfy all a man's wants and desires.

Man is an animal and I don't care how well-educated a person is, how famous they are, they still go the way of the flesh. When a woman is right for a man in bed, she has the perfect and the greatest control. But there has to be an appeal, something unique about the woman. If you have a scale for judging good between one and ten, and the woman gets ten for her face, she is already 33 percent desirable. A ten body is a Raquel Welch body. Yvette Mimeux has the best body I have ever seen on a woman. A woman shoud be slim, but not skinny, with a good pair of legs. Altogether beautiful women are better in bed; they are not afraid of men because men have rarely caused them problems.

I couldn't touch a girl unless I know her. I have to know there is no shit in her blood. Also, the slightest remark can trurn me off at the beginning, like, "Who the fuck needs you?" A lot depends on a woman's experience, her fears and desires. The secret of good sex is to be uninhibited and to reciprocate in bed. Another things that makes a woman good is the way she touches a man. There is a way some women touch which is like saying, "I am the dessert you have earned after buying me that expensive meal." Also, if you touch a woman and she pulls back, forget it; she may pull back at a crucial moment in bed.

Conversation matters and so does mystique. If I go over to a woman's place and she appears stark naked, there is nothing exciting for me. But if she appears in a black negligee, then the male who gets pleasure out of conquest wants to remove it. The greatest charm a woman possesses is being very feminine. I don't want to screw someone I am in competition with. I don't like to be pursued. I like to call the tune, and if I get lucky, great.

My profession attracts a lot of women to me: TV has created an aura of glamor around the detective. But women are only a part of a man's life. I could exist without a woman. A man who is in the arena, making money, traveling all over the world—why should he settle for one woman? The first one he meets may not be as good in bed as the last.

JOHN MARSHALL

Film Producer

Film producer John Marshall and I had breakfast at his hotel in Beverly Hills, and when I told him about Warren Beatty, he tried to contact him and discover why he thought my question was so terrible.

Warren was away, but Muhammad Ali, who is starring in Ali, *the film of his life which John Marshall is producing, was not. So I asked Muhammad Ali my question and he said: "What makes a woman G.I.B? It is against my Islamic teachings and my morals to talk about people in bed."*

John Marshall has produced TV specials and documentaries throughout the world. As a personal manager, he has helped shape the careers of Nina van Pallandt and Richard Harris.

Initial sexual attraction between a man and a woman is still physical. It may be the way she laughs, the way she stands, the way she holds her cigarette, or the way she may smile or walk. Obviously, if you enter a room and you see a girl and you are attracted to her instantly, then it has to be physical. You don't necessarily analyze it, and it can easily be shattered—particularly in the film business—when she opens her mouth. Very often the quietest girls turn out to be the very best in bed, rather like still waters tending to run deep. A lot of girls flaunt sex, walk into a bar, attract a lot of attention, and probably aren't that good.

I think that if a woman is sexual, she can be blond, brunette, small, tall, thin, or fat. Sex is a combination of physical, mental, and visual. A woman who is capable of making a man feel he is a man in bed, that she appreciates what he is doing, is the best. If a man is not a selfish lover, he likes to know that she has had an orgasm. Some girls take longer than others, but that doesn't make them less good, just more inhibited, less experienced. Experience makes a woman good; practice makes perfect.

What is sexually attractive to one man won't be attractive to another, thank God, otherwise women would have a very rough time, and so would men. In this business a lot of women go to bed with men they are not attracted to because they are often attracted by the status, rather than the man. Actresses are attracted to producers and agents; they may tell you sex is *not* a means to an end, but usually it is. People imagine that because a girl is a well-known actress, representing sex to thousands of men on the screen, she will be fantastic in bed. I can think of a number of well-known actresses I've slept with who one might think would be good, but who were awful in bed, because actresses are very narcissistic. It is ten to one that a pretty girl working in an office is better.

KATE

Girl Friday

Kate is a thirty-five-year-old New York girl Friday. When I met her she was newly divorced and undergoing assertiveness training.

I was seventeen when I got married. My husband was fifteen years older than I and very selfish in bed. Right from the start I had to make him believe that he was king of the road, or rather, the bed. I did whatever he asked because I wanted to be good for him. I was a virgin, and everything I learned about sex and being good in bed was what my husband taught me—what pleased *him*.

If I wanted to touch his face, but he didn't want me to, I didn't. If he wanted to make love for a long time—and I didn't—we did.

He wanted to be superior, so I had to forever succumb. I didn't know myself as a woman, so I was very pleased to please him. It was always one-way traffic in bed. I did get pleasure out of sex because he was very skillful, but all the time he made me feel he was being kind and generous to let me have any pleasure at all. I was good for him, but only because I did everything he wanted.

Since my divorce, I had one affair and I started it on the same sexual principle of pleasing the man. But one day Harry mentioned my attitude and said, "I want you to please yourself, and to tell me anything you want to do in bed." That was when I realized that I had fallen into the same sexual pattern as with my husband and was in danger of ending up frustrated and angry. But we talked about it, as Harry has no insecurity hang-ups. I am beginning to ask for what I want in bed, even to the point of acting out my fantasies. At last I know that I don't have to give up my desires in bed, and that I can talk about sex.

My telling Harry what I want in bed made *him* tell *me* what he wanted. He is very powerful and masculine, but one day he told me that he wanted me to tie him up and master him. I thought it was very kinky, and I felt a bit scared, but I still did it to please him. Except it was in a different way from how I did things for my husband, because Harry does things to please *me*, as well, so we are equal. If a man said to me, "Are you good in bed?" I would still find it hard to answer. Anyway, as people become more aware of themselves, it shouldn't matter if they are good or not.

LYNN L.

Personal Assistant

Lynn L. has been the personal assistant to one of the world's most famous male sex symbols, and is currently girl Friday to a best-selling author. She is slim, vivacious, attractive, and in her thirties.

I lost my virginity in the fifties, and sex has changed all over the world since then. I thought all a woman had to do was lie there. The boys I went with didn't tell me anything different. I don't think women were expected to be good in the fifties, because men had no respect for a girl who wasn't a virgin, although they tried their best to make her not be one. Nowadays, it's quite the opposite, although I suppose there are still some sick guys around who are looking for virgins.

There is a difference between what *really* makes a woman good in bed and what a *man* thinks makes a woman good in bed. A man thinks a woman is good if she doesn't make any waves—does whatever the man wants, doesn't ask any questions about anyone else, or about where he is going, or when she is going to see him again. I think a man is happiest if a woman doesn't feel any emotion for him. So if a woman asked me for advice on how to be good in bed on the *man's* terms, I would advise her to do whatever the man wants her to do and to pretend that she loves it all.

A man wants a woman to be a whore in bed, and to try lots of tricks, but I don't think men go for a woman who is desperate to be fucked nonstop, because then they get tired. A man doesn't always like a woman who wants him just for sex. Some time ago, I had a relationship with a man who was a shit—never showing up on time, and lying to me, but I survived because he was technically so fantastic in bed. Then one day I decided I had had enough of the way he treated me, so I called him up and said, ''Listen, I'm not going to call you any more. But I want to tell you something. I think you're a really good fuck, so if you're interested in just fucking, you call me, and if I'm here, fine.'' He was quite taken aback. A little while later he called and arrived over on time, treated me nicely, but was *terrible* in bed, and came in a minute. It was as if he knew that all I was interested in was the sex, and therefore he didn't have to try to hold me emotionally by being good.

I have changed a lot in bed. I even change from month to month. I believe that for a woman to be good in bed for *herself,* she should fully enjoy what she does in bed and not feel she has to do everything to please the man, although sometimes I like to just please, or give head, and not get anything in return. I think that's a great big turn-on. I have learned that my obligation in bed is really just to me. So, in my own definition of what makes a woman good in bed, I am good if I enjoy myself—and I don't get full enjoyment out of sex unless I come. There were times when I knew that according to the man's definition I was good in bed—but not according to my own, because I didn't have an orgasm.

Unless they care about you, men don't give a damn if you really come or not, so you can do all the faking you want to gratify them, to make them feel like big shots. I must admit that from time to time I fake in bed. Usually I fake when a guy is taking ages to come, and I have completely lost interest in the middle, either because I couldn't feel him, or he wasn't making the right moves. I would never fake a big, tremendous orgasm, but I just shudder a bit and say, ''Oh, I've come,'' to get the whole thing over with.

After you have slept with a man a few times you can sense what he is going to enjoy, but most guys don't admit the things they want up front. You have to kind of get friendly with them and say, "What do you like? I'll do anything once." But I don't like anal sex, so if I am asked, I say, "I would be very happy to do it, but first we'll get a dildo and we'll stick it up your ass, and we'll see how you like it." They can go to men for that.

I am different with every guy I go to bed with. There are a number of men who think I am fantastic in bed and would recommend me—in fact I know they *have* recommended me. But there are others who think, "Jesus, why bother?" My being good depends on how I feel about the man, but also on what he brings out in me. If a man can make me trust him, then I will be much more open and much more loving and giving. When two people are in love, the sex will be fantastic. My great sexual fantasy is that the man I am in bed with is terribly in love with me; that turns me on far more than any other sexual fantasy.

No matter how fantastic a woman is in bed, she has to have much more for a man to come back to her, because thousands of women are good in bed, especially here in Hollywood, where sex is so cheap and so easy to get. A man can go anyplace—take a walk on the Sunset Strip, go and get a newspaper from Schwab's, or wherever—and find a woman who will go to bed with him. So I don't think there is any correlation between a woman being good in bed and the man coming back to her. Most men think they're such hot shit, but they're not. It's how *you* feel about sex, how much *you* enjoy it that matters, because you can't use sex to make a man stay with you.

JENNIFER LEIGH

Porno Star

Jennifer Leigh, porno star, appeared in the black porno film Lialeh *and is in her late twenties.*

I think I am good because I have never had any sexual complaints. I try to satisfy a man to the full extent. I know what I want to get out of sex, and you only get what you put into it.

I like every affair to be a love affair and not just a fuck. It need only happen once or twice, but I put a lot of effort into an affair. I spend a lot of time on the mood: incense, soft lights, music, candles. Creating the right atmosphere makes me good. Some men get turned on by silky nighties; others like baby dolls. I try to stay innocent-looking, because men like that look. I know what a man wants the moment I meet him. I am good by intuition.

I don't have many affairs. Most of the men I meet turn into friends. I like sex to a certain degree. I like that flow, that energy, of two people merging—their eyes, their minds, and their beings—into each other. I drift into a man. I stop liking sex, though, when it becomes a task. I can go comfortably for half an hour, but there are men who constantly grab and touch and aren't sensuous; they just fuck and sweat. I like men who are soft and mellow; they stop, talk, and then get back into it. A constant feeling of being a machine makes me turn off, so then I ask the man to leave.

I went through two months on a bisexual trip, and I figured that after experiencing both sexes, I was ready for anything. But the bisexuality bothered me and it passed, although I do think that having been with other women can help me to teach men what is best for me, because a woman really knows what turns a woman on. Whereas men often fumble, unless they are really experienced.

If I had to tell another woman how to be good in bed, I would tell her to learn oral sex. I learned through watching *Deep Throat*. I can come by giving a man oral sex. Just to look at his face, and to see how turned on he is. I know when to stop and what to do. There is usually a slight pulsation before they come, then I stop and we have sex.

Now that I am older I have become better in bed. I have learned a lot. Being good in bed is something you learn; you aren't born with it. I don't do things I don't want in bed because I am just trying to be good. I need to be free in bed to do what I want. I know how to satisfy a man. A total body massage, done slowly all over, is great for the man. I would wait, if I didn't know a man too well, before asking for everything I want in bed. If I love someone, I do everything, not just for the sake of being good, but to please him.

B.L.

Gangster

I wanted a gangster in the book, and I found B.L. via police connections. There's very little else to tell, because I was told very little about B.L.—just his initials. While I waited for him in my apartment I had fantasies of becoming a gangster's moll, but the interview was brief, and now I can't remember anything about him except that he had frighteningly big hands.

A woman has to have the desire to get balled; without that, you can forget the whole game. Some women get into bed, and they're so preoccupied, so wrapped up in themselves, that they make you feel they're going to do you a favor—that they're bestowing something on you. Women like that are not in bed to get balled. Women like that are using sex as a foothold to get what they want from a man, or to reward him for something.

There has to be something about the woman that turns you on immediately when you look at her. I don't think that has anything to do with state of mind. It doesn't matter whether a woman is tall or thin, lean, muscular, or round, but of course you don't want anything that is homely or absurd in any way.

Talkers are bad in bed: the girl who is trying to show me how worldly and sophisticated she is. Talking all the time, right up to sex, and during it, really trying to impress a man. A woman like that will laugh and giggle during sex, but she is just trying to prove that she is blase and knows all about sex.

If you have had a good experience with a girl the first time, then it will definitely get better, definitely improve. The first encounter or two is feeling out the ground work. The girl who says to you, "Gee, I've just met you," and doesn't want to let go, inhibits the hell out of a man.

I've always found that you will get a lot further with a girl if you let her know openly that you are not looking to get married. So, then she does not have to worry about doing things in bed because she is afraid that you will be put off by her. It doesn't matter if a woman refuses something I want in bed if it is something small. Like I might say to her, "Let's take a bath together," and she might say, "No." I think about the only refusal that could turn me off is when a woman has a frigid attitude and feels and acts as if everything is dirty.

The ideal woman in bed is aggressive at times, shy at times, bold at times, and certainly isn't damn predictable. I hate a woman who every night puts on a robe, gets into bed, waits for you to give her a kiss; the same moves, the same sort of thing over and over again—that wears out quickly. It's the woman who comes bouncing into the room now and again to get *you* who's interesting. That's the kind of woman who's good in bed.

I just don't have a *modus operandi*. I rarely go out and pick up a girl and take her home to bed. If I have an evening with her, and enjoy it, then I want to get started. It doesn't matter if it takes a woman a long time to come. A lot of girls are very hot and come in a few minutes, but that can be very bad if the woman decides to quit right away. Then the sex is all over. The woman who says, "Oh, dear, it took me a long time" is also bad—the woman who starts playing around with her own psyche, becomes preoccupied with her own organs and her own orgasm. But most of all, and worst of all, is a woman who fakes in bed. A woman has to be natural—she has to deal with sex as if it were nothing more than an appetite, like food.

JOHNNY BRISTOL

Record Producer

Johnny Bristol is a very glamorous thirty-six-year-old Black record producer, singer, and songwriter. He has produced records for Diana Ross and the Supremes, Gladys Knight and the Pips, and Junior Walker and the All-Stars, and was nominated for a Grammy for his song "Hang On In There Baby."

When I look at a woman, I judge whether she is good in bed because of her air of freshness and lack of inhibition—you can tell by conversation. You can look at a woman and say, "She is sexy," but just because she *looks* perfect out of bed, she may not know what to do with the tools once she is in bed Just because a carpenter has a hammer, it doesn't mean he knows how to hammer in a nail. A woman can be sexy and still not be good in bed—there is always a certain excitement about being in bed with a woman who is attractive, or physically well-endowed—it appeals to a man's animal instincts.

I get turned off if a woman sits down *before* we go to bed and says, "This is what I want you to do: one, two, three, four, five." There is a way of telling a man what you want. Communication in sex is vital. Women can sometimes tell you physically what they want or don't want. I understand if a woman refuses something in bed; her head is just not there and a woman should never be forced into a sexual situation she is not ready for.

An experienced woman is good because she has learned techniques, but I think that if a woman has not had the advantages of techniques, she can still reach a climax and enjoy sex. Perhaps she would love to know more things to do in bed, because desire is driving her crazy inside. A man should be aware of this, and where the woman is at mentally, to be able to say, "I know her problem" and guide her so that she will feel comfortable. Feeling comfortable makes a woman let go, and letting go makes a woman good. A woman who is free doesn't have to be experienced, but has to be free enough in her mind to take advantage of my experience.

I think fantasies are very important as well. If you find a woman you can talk to about your fantasies while you make love, you are at ease with her, because then you trust each other enough to share your fantasies. Most women are still scared of telling their fantasies in case the man will think she gets more pleasure from her fantasies than from him.

There are women who enjoy sex to its fullest, but still can't reach an orgasm because they are wrapped up in the whole experience, the total thing, and not the orgasm. Their pleasure can be derived from what they receive from the man and from his pleasure. If a man *cares,* it is up to him to be patient and communicate with the woman, but he may not always know if a woman has reached an orgasm—some women reach a climax and don't physically let it out, but still enjoy sex, while others are fighting themselves not to let it out because they don't want to be embarrassed, which is ridiculous. The hippest part of making love is freedom—to let it out. Why hide it? If I am making it happen, let go.

A woman can always let you know, "That's where it's at, right there, this is the pocket, stay right there and if you stay right there, we are going to have a touchdown." Many men try to prove their manhood by how hard and how deep they can go, but then it's over, they get confused, and it is all due to selfishness. God gave woman one of the most fantastic things (as far as sex is concerned)—the ability to reach an orgasm forever; as long as a man can find a pocket, a woman can let it out, so it's up to the man to find it.

Women think they have a fixed time span, so when they reach one orgasm quickly they are shocked and amazed. Women create this fixed span when they masturbate. They think, "Five minutes here, and then I will get an orgasm." Not because that is their physical makeup, but because their minds are controlling them. A woman could really lie there for twenty minutes and let her mind go; then I bet she could just go on and on having orgasms.

I think there are certain levels of orgasm for a woman; there are orgasms they have never reached before, but all of a sudden, one moment, one man, one time, takes a woman to a place she has never been before. There is no limit. Women must never think they can go no higher, because that ruins sex for the man, and no matter what he does, or how tender he is, he won't be able to give her an orgasm.

No matter how patient he is, it won't happen if she has already fixed in her mind that one orgasm is all she can reach. There is more to sex than that. An orgasm for a man should just be the icing on the cake. If he doesn't get it, fine, plain cake is equally good. Man is born with the ability to make love—it's easy to become erect, but some women still say, "You get it up and I'll get in it"—which makes sex simple, but *that* is not being good in bed.

MICHAEL McCOWAN

Tycoon

Michael McCowan is a forty-two-year-old tycoon who owns a yacht and homes in both America and Europe.

I had my first experience when I was nine, with a sixteen-year-old, and I liked it. It tickled.

I think I can tell by looking at a woman if she is good in bed. I'm really into sex. I really enjoy it. When I was single, and I had my boat down at the marina, I went to bed with as many different women as I could—fat ones, skinny ones, tall ones, short ones, stocky ones, loud ones, quiet ones—so I have a composite woman who is good in bed.

First off, a woman who has a very large mouth will have a wide vagina—that's a fact—take my word for it. A woman who has a small mouth generally will have a small, tight vagina. (I base all of this on experience with four to five hundred women.) Of course a small vagina isn't always good.

If a woman is small and dry, and has a tight socket, it's not very much fun to make love to her. Women vary from very dry to just absolutely dripping when you can tell they're excited.

The youger the woman, the least amount of sexual hang-ups she has. When you get to women thirty, thirty-five, and older, they are more difficult, they are more hung up and they want to know where the relationship is going, what it means to me, what is happening. I like slender, long-legged women. I like women with large breasts, but sometimes big breasts are far less sensitive than small breasts. Whether the woman has large or small breasts, it's how much she gets turned on when they're caressed or touched that matters.

I love a woman who has pretty feet. I really like pretty feet and nice ankles, good, long legs with good calves, and an ass that just tucks under. If anything at all, I would be an ass man. I like an ass that comes out and is well-rounded. I love a neck with a slope, and pretty hands, and a satin-smooth feel to the skin. Also good teeth. I think that we Americans have a tooth fetish.

A woman could have everything, but if she sprayed her hair, and perfumed it up, she wouldn't be right for me, I like hair to feel soft and be natural; I like bright eyes—green or blue—and a woman with some creative talent—writing, painting, interior decorating. I don't like dumb women, I like a woman who has something to say, but who doesn't always agree with me. She has to like foreplay and kissing. I love to kiss. You don't always have to be in love with a woman, sometimes it's good just to have an animal fuck.

I like aggressive women. That turns me on. A woman who lets you know she wants to make love. She'll grab you by the joint, or she'll kiss you on the ear and say, "Let's go to bed." I enjoy having a partner who does that. I like a woman who is sexual. Some women who are very sexual can be totally animal—they just want to fuck, and they are not sensuous. A sensuous woman wants to take time to make love.

Most men have to please a woman to get pleased. They feel like failures unless the woman they are with climaxes. I have known women to have climaxes until they are totally exhausted; they keep coming. They might have thirty or forty climaxes before you have one. But sometimes it's good to work for the woman to have an orgasm, too. I like a woman who is into sex, really likes it, and I don't think I can be fooled by a woman who is just doing it because she thinks it's the thing to do, or who doesn't have a climax and tries to fake. I like spontaneity in making love. I like to make love on the floor, in the sink, in the shower. One of the best experiences I've ever had was by a lake in the tall grass when it was raining. I couldn't get the grass stains off my body for three weeks.

My kind of woman wouldn't refuse anything in bed, because she would believe, as I do, that there's nothing bad in bed. If you want to stick it in her ear, that's not wrong. Most women like being eaten, but there are some women who are bashful about it and will either pull your head or push it. Then you will have to talk about it in a disguised way, not while you are in bed, but the next day, cautiously.

I have known two out of a hundred women who don't give head, but to me, it's part of the sex act. I don't get turned on by anal sex, but some women do like it. I've met a few who want to do it that way. I've seen a lot more threesomes and bisexuality nowadays in California. I think women are more bisexual than men. Women are better able to handle a bisexual relationship than men. Every man has had some kind of homosexual relationship, though. I can remember being with little boys when I was little, and we would look at each other's pee-pees and feel them.

My ideal woman in bed would be totally into me. (I am old enough to realize this would never be true.) She could meet James Caan or Warren Beatty—they would want her—but she would be totally impervious to them—because she had me.

SANDY FAWKES

Journalist

Sandy Fawkes is one of England's best known fashion and feature journalists. She is divorced with three children and lives in Hollywood, where she is currently writing a screenplay.

Desire makes a woman good in bed, and desire is wanting a particular man, a particular body, regardless if he is good in bed or not. I wasn't instinctively good; I had to learn from lots of different men, from pleasing them. I married the first man I went to bed with, and stayed faithful to him for ten years. I was one sexual personality for those ten years, a paragon (as you have to be if you have three children under the age of five). I am delighted to say that I got out-maneuvered one day; through that man I found a new delight in sex and decided that I wished to pursue it.

My experience grew with my desire to be experienced. I made some terrible mistakes that give me the shudders today. You do get yourself in some awful situations when you are learning anything, and particularly when you are learning about sex. You lack discretion, the strength to say you don't want to do something in bed, because you feel that you are very inexperienced; so you force yourself and get into situations from which there is no escape with dignity.

Now I usually get what I want in bed. I am not into whips and chains, and if somebody did produce whips and chains I would just tell them to fuck off—I would never be that scared of losing anybody and I would never want anybody that much. Sex is an area of my own. I don't want threesomes; that is not a game I want to play.

Giving a man oral sex makes a woman good because a lot of other women don't like doing it. A part of being good has to do with one's pelvic muscles being articulate, with all the muscles, including the vaginal muscles, kept very trim and firm. Any kind of dancing keeps it all going. But anyway, if you want a body, none of it is revolting. I enjoy sex thoroughly, and when you are relaxed enough there is no need for verbal communication in bed.

Orgasm doesn't worry me; I come very easily and if I don't, it is because of some kind of tension. But I wouldn't worry if I didn't come. I would just say, "Let's try again later." I think that a lot of men don't know if a woman has come or not, and the ones who do generally understand. I enjoy sex enormously and I didn't at first. If I do get out-maneuvered, and one obviously does, it is just a matter of settling back and enjoying it. Basically I go to bed when I want to, and with whom I want to, but if I don't find anybody I want to go to bed with, I go without.

I am self-confident in bed, and I really enjoy sex. I think my sexual self-confidence arises partially from my job. When one is confident of one's welcome as a human being, it doesn't matter if one is overweight. I happen to have a voluptuous figure that goes in and out, rather more out than in. Obviously, if I am standing next to some slender five-foot-seven blonde, aged twenty-four or twenty-five, I don't exactly feel like a magnificent physical specimen, but if I open my mouth and start talking, my mind is well-furnished.

Some men have given the game away afterwards, that they have screwed me as a status thing. One man I went out with told me he had gone for a walk along the cliffs afterwards and said out loud, "I've fucked Sandy Fawkes." I thought that was so funny, because many years ago, when I started out, I use to think men were more glamorous if they were famous. An American girl defined it as star-balling, and I still refer to that time as my star-balling phase, so it was funny to see that I have become a status symbol.

I am sure I make it clear to men that there are no strings attached to me; the last thing I want is somebody turning up with a suitcase, having left his wife, and the last thing I want is a man who rings me up at work to ask what I am doing. And men to whom one is an achievement are likely to be waiting for telephone calls, letters, and in general, to be commanded. Successful men are obviously different—they look for equality of relationship, however temporary, when they find a successful woman. They are very sure of themselves and are usually my equal mentally. Successful men are not necessarily better in bed—just more alluring for the pre-bed games. They also know I am not going to be sitting by the phone crying and that I am going to take the relationship absolutely as it is given, on the day, or the week, however long it lasts.

I am very good at letting go of men. But I got to that point through being desperately wounded. It's not that I let go—I just don't let anybody near me, I don't let them infiltrate. And I think it makes life a lot simpler. I wish I had learned that a lot younger.

Sexual possessiveness is really harmful, because then you feel you are of less worth if somebody you care about has clambered into bed with another woman. If you know there is always somebody else, somewhere else, you feel at ease with yourself and become more tolerant and less demanding in bed.

Sex is something to be enjoyed, like a good meal when I want it. That may sound very masculine, and I know I have developed a very masculine attitude to men and to sex. It suits me fine at this stage, professionally, and in every way, but my whole attitude would be wiped out if I fell in love.

SIDNEY SHELDON

Author

Sidney Sheldon is the best-selling author of The Other Side of Midnight *and* A Stranger in the Mirror.

There are a lot of silly superstitions about sex, like ''Women who wear glasses are no fun in bed''—but in reality it is the glamor women, the sexpots, the movie stars, who are less good in bed. Women who are plain and unsexy-looking can be marvelous, and beautiful women can be terrible. In my bachelor days I went out with a lot of beautiful movie stars and models, but you never have much fun in bed with girls like that. They're so concerned about their appearance, their clothes, and think about themselves constantly. They don't want their hair messed up when they go to bed with you, and are totally preoccupied with themselves and their own pleasure—never thinking about the man, never giving to him, just selfish in bed.

Physical things matter. Even though I don't think there is a physical type that is good in bed, I do think it is important for a girl to have a good body. That is a turn-on for me, just as it turns women on to have a man with a good body. A body in good shape is good in bed, so even a woman of fifty or sixty can be very sexy, if she's also in good shape.

I think women are more sexy as they get older. Experience

helps in bed, but some women are just naturally very sensual at any age, whereas other women could not be sensual in a million years. Basically it has to be *in* you—you have to be born a sensuous person. If a woman is a giving person, the chances are that she will also be a sensual, sexual person. A giving woman is instinctively a very sexual woman, who wants to give the man pleasure.

Today there is a kind of philosophy that if a man doesn't come to an orgasm every time it is not terribly important, because the idea is to please the woman, so a man feels that he has failed in bed if he hasn't given the woman an orgasm. However, for many women having an orgasm doesn't really matter. Noelle, my heroine in *The Other Side of Midnight,* is that kind of a woman.

I invented Noelle to be the prototype of the woman who is good in bed. She never has pleasure out of sex except once, with the man she loves. Otherwise, she uses sex deliberately to get what she wants. She is cold and calculating and is really a courtesan in the tradition of the great courtesans trained just to please men. Noelle trained herself like a geisha girl to please a man by concentrating on giving him pleasure and forgetting her own. Women whose only concern is to bring pleasure to a man make great bed partners. Sex like that, without emotion, can sometimes be a very pleasurable thing, and every man should take advange of it if ever he gets the opportunity to go to bed with a courtesan.

Otherwise, the ideal woman in bed is a woman who cares for the man as much as he cares for her. Then sex between them should be marvelous and equal, because sex should never be to the benefit of one person. The most satisfying sex in the world is still when two people are in love, make love, because then the sex becomes something other than just a mechanical function.

BOB FREDERICKS
Publicist

Bob Fredericks is the Hollywood publicist for Warner Brothers. Recent films he has publicized include Barry Lyndon, All the President's Men, *and* A Star is Born.

I fantasize if a woman is going to be good in bed when I meet her. If she is the type that turns me on and fits my mold, I fantasize that everything else is going to be perfect about her in bed. The mold changes, but over the years I most desire the Cybill Shepherd type of California girl: long blonde hair, tanned skin. I like a happy medium in bed, not too thin or too plump. I can't imagine what it would be like to make love to the *Vogue* type of model—like making love to a broomstick, I should imagine. When I make love to someone, I want to know that I am holding her.

When you first meet a lady, the important factor is what she can bring to the experience that maybe you have never experienced before, or that you have experienced before and enjoyed. Once you get to know her, you may tire of each other, so then, no matter what happens in bed, the woman can never be good, because she is not the woman you want. If you are in love with her, she can probably be a lot less good in bed—less active—but will still seem good, because you love her. I equate the woman who is good with the active, imaginative woman.

Some women don't have orgasms easily. It is always important to me for the woman to reach an orgasm, but a lot of women have told me that even though they never—or rarely—reach one, that never lessens the experience for them. But I have met women who can put a man through all kinds of things in bed before they have an orgasm. Maybe a man has to go on for an hour, till he gets very tired and wants to tell the woman, "enough"—but if you care about pleasing her, you try, or else you leave. Then perhaps, if a man knows that the next time he sees the lady he will have to go through that same routine to satisfy her, he may not feel equal to it and will think, "I am too tired to spend all that time and trouble to give her an orgasm."

JANE LOVELLE

Starlet

Jane Lovelle is a very beautiful rising young Hollywood actress.

I think I am good in bed. I don't worry about things other women are doing in bed that I may not know about. I can't know everything about sex, but that still doesn't stop me from being good at what I do know. I believe that being good in bed is ambiguous. You can sometimes transcend off the bed spiritually and emotionally, and that is much more important than just being technically good. I could talk about acrobatics and sexual techniques, but everything depends on who you are in bed with, and how much you value his opinion of what makes a woman good in bed.

There is a difference between what is good and what a man likes. I could suck a man off and he would like it, but that wouldn't mean that I was good at doing it; men are really very easy to satisfy. The only time you can really judge if you are good in bed is if you are in bed with a man who has a problem like impotency. Then, if you help him to get over it, you could possibly call yourself good, except in that case good would really be another name for tenacity and patience in bed.

I always appear mysterious when I meet a man—not on purpose—it just happens. But the first time in bed with someone is tedious. You enjoy it, but there are a lot of tensions. The sex is just not as good as it becomes, because you don't know each other well enough. I sometimes think of the other girls he has fucked, the scent stains on his cock, and that no matter how much he has washed they will never come off.

I need fantasies to be good. I can't divorce emotions from the physical side of sex because I never just feel physically horny; there are a lot of images that go with it. If I feel that I am not emotionally involved I have to create an image around the man, a fantasy. I have fantasies that I am the mistress of the house, and I am making the male servants have sex with me. I am totally different in bed with every man: with some men I am like a whore—with others the sex transcends an earthly experience.

The main thing in sex is independence; I complain if I don't get an orgasm in bed. I go on like a trade union and say, "Come on. Fifty-fifty. I don't do this just to please you. If you can't please me, then there is something wrong. We will have to discuss it." Then *they* wonder if they are good in bed. But I wouldn't react like that if I didn't know a man well.

Failing in bed is subjecting yourself to a man, doing everything to please him, so you don't even realize why you are doing it or why you are in bed. That happens to girls who go to bed as a natural course, in the same way as they have coffee after a meal. I believe that you should play hard-to-get in an emotional context. I always have confidence when I go to bed with someone because I don't sleep around, so that when I go to bed with someone, I know we like each other. Therefore, sex is a natural extension of the relationship. I have never fucked anyone without having a relationship first, which is why I never feel sexually inadequate, because the sex is not the be-all-and-end-all of everything. I don't want to fuck someone I don't know.

ERIC DRACHE

Professional Poker Player

Eric Drache is one of Las Vegas' leading professional poker players. He has been playing poker for twelve years, and he has been known to win over a hundred thousand dollars in one night. Eric is in his thirties, an attractive, quiet, gentle, All-American boy. After I met him, I was playing the slot machines at the Dunes in Las Vegas, and I won the jackpot. Very excited, I rushed over to Eric, clutching five dollars in dimes. He congratulated me, then went back to the table, where he had just lost fifty thousand dollars.

A group of guys always sit round the poker table and look at the girls walking through the casino. There are always comments like, "I bet she would be good in bed." It's usually quite the opposite—the type who looks good has probably been to bed with so many men that sex has become completely boring for her, whereas the innocent, sweet-looking girl can be a hell of a lot better in bed. Although a woman has to be attractive before I *want* to go to bed in the first place, and I like a woman with a big bust, I can't tell if she is good in bed by just looking at her. I can tell, though, if she *wants* to go to bed.

A woman is good in bed if she comes; no matter how liberal she is, or how well she gives head, somehow it seems as if she wasn't good in bed if she doesn't have an orgasm. She doesn't always have to come quickly though; sometimes a quick orgasm is just a preparation for bigger orgasms. A guy is happy to have a girl who takes half an hour before coming, because it is a symbol of virility for the man to be able to last long in bed, so when a girl comes quickly, the man has no opportunity to show off his staying power. But then again, a woman isn't necessarily bad if she doesn't come at all.

I don't think a woman is less good if she refuses something in bed. I don't particularly want a woman to be obsequious. I wouldn't like her to do something that *she* didn't want to do, although I would probably try to persuade her if I thought she had never considered it. But I would never force her. I like a woman to ask for what she wants in bed. I don't remember ever being turned off or shocked by something a woman has asked for. I know that a few women wanted head and were afraid to ask for it. I didn't think they were less good, just shy.

If I could create the ideal woman to be good in bed she would have the opposite knack from a prostitute. A prostitute really has to be totally submissive, do everything a man wants, and also has to have the ability to fake an orgasm. I don't want any of that. In many ways a woman of forty and a girl of seventeen can be very similar in bed. In Las Vegas we get a lot of forty-year-old divorcees who have had very little sex, just like some girls of seventeen, so then sex is just as much a novelty for the forty-year-old as it is for the seventeen-year-old, and I think being good in bed is finding sex a novelty and appreciating it.

DEE

Dancer

Dee is a Bluebell Girl from the Paris Lido. The Bluebell Girls are celebrated as the tallest and most beautiful dancers in the world.

As a Bluebell Girl, I have my pick of men, but I think I am still learning a lot about sex and ought to experience more different men. I tend to go out with a guy for a long time, and therefore, at the age of twenty-two, I haven't had much experience. I don't think I can generally say, "I am good in bed," but I know I am not bad in bed because I respond to a man—and being bad is not responding, being insensitive, and being afraid to ask for what you want. At first, though, I was scared to ask a guy for what I wanted in bed; I kept thinking, "Should I do this? Should I do that?" But I am getting more confidence, and confidence does make you better in bed.

I sell sex every night. We go on stage and it's all crotch bumps and G-strings. That gives you confidence in your body, and I take that confidence with me to bed. I am not a shy person and I take my clothes off easily, being a dancer. We all walk around backstage with just little G-strings on covering our *frous*. Some of the girls do hate the idea of even a gay guy bursting into the dressing room and seeing their breasts, but I think that's silly.

I am very supple because I am a dancer, and I am more aware of my body. Even just walking down the street I am conscious of my muscles and the way I walk, so I am not stiff or scared of new positions. Having to dance with people during the show is a sexual thing—it's doing something with your body in relationship to other people. For example, we do a very sexual *pas de deux* in the show with just G-strings on. I am not saying that dancers are better in bed, because you have some very inhibited dancers—but once they overcome their inhibitions they ought to be better in bed.

I used to worry about being good in bed, and I think every woman does. Sometimes when a relationship went wrong, I would wonder if one of the reasons was because I hadn't been good in bed. But, on the other hand, you change with different guys, and the main thing is to be turned on to each different guy you're with. I think kids who have grown up in a household deprived of love are less likely to be good in bed. I did grow up in a household with a lot of love. I was lucky to be able to show love, so I'm not afraid of showing my affection to anyone. If I go out with a guy, I am not afraid to kiss him in public.

My upbringing was strict, but when I got away from home, I lost my virginity when I was nineteen. I went to bed with a guy I didn't really know. He was gorgeous and he really seduced me, but it didn't work out and the whole thing was a mess. But I still lost my shyness with him, although I was a bit tense because I was worried about getting pregnant.

Although I am not shy anymore, I have not quite gotten to the stage of acting out all my fantasies in bed. If I am really in love with a man, and we know each other and we have a good mental relationship, I don't worry about asking for things (but I still wouldn't go to bed with a man the first week I met him). After that, I might, and I'd ask for what I wanted. Sometimes even in long-term relationships people don't tell each other what they want in bed, so it's a great big hassle trying to guess. I used to go through all of that, but I don't anymore.

Now I tell the guy what makes me come, he does it, and then I do come. It's all a matter of telling a man. Telling a man helps to make a woman good. It helps to make her excited and makes her come, and then if she comes and gets more excited, he gets excited. The whole thing of sex is a great big cycle.

If I had to give advice on being good in bed, I would tell a girl to relax. If she's with a young guy who is not experienced, I would say good luck, but if she's with an older guy who could teach her, I would just tell her to be open-minded and to do what he suggests. Be honest and say, "Look, I don't know what it's about. You show me."

I have a few inhibitions left, but not many. I haven't done anything very kinky yet. I have never done a threesome, and I don't know if I would or not. A lot depends on what the guy was like—whether I was in love with him or not. I would give things like an orgy a chance. I have never been asked to one, but I would give it a go, and if I didn't like it—I would leave. What the hell. Above all, I believe in being open-minded about sex, and not having too many inhibitions.

We talk about sex all the time at work, especially in our row of five girls, and our dresser is even worse than us. But we never really talk about what makes us good in bed. One of the girls will come in and say, "I've just had the most fantastic sex—oh, it was so good, so fantastic last night." But they never define what *they* did to be good. I think we mean satisfying ourselves and coming when we say, "It was good." I think it's self-satisfaction that women boast about—not what *they* did in bed, not that they were good, but that the experience itself was good. Men say, "I did it eight times," but women don't say anything like that. They just say, "The sex was fantastic—*it* was very good," not, "*I* was very good."

BOB AYLOTT

Photographer

Bob Aylott is a twenty-six-year-old photographer of glamor women, pin-ups, and beauty queens.

Chemistry makes a woman good, and chemistry is difficult to describe. Chemistry happens even before you talk to someone. You can recognize it by looking at a woman across a crowded room. Whatever a woman does in bed is all a waste of time if she is not enjoying sex. What really turns a guy on is women who really enjoy sex. It doesn't matter how long they take to come, as long as they are enjoying themselves.

A woman has to have a sense of humor about sex. When you think about it, it's nothing serious. So many disastrous things happen in bed. A guy might be pissed and not able to get it up, so then the woman has to work very hard, and if she looks at it lightheartedly, that helps. A woman doesn't have to wear anything in bed, just a smile. I also like a woman with a bum like a plum; it helps to lift them up a bit so they are easier to get at.

The woman who is good in bed has to have the motions of the ocean. You can pick out the girls who are going to be good in bed by the way they dance. A woman has to be a great mover. And if you are dancing with a woman, the way she moves her body can conquer you right there on the dance floor. There is nothing worse than a girl who just lies in bed and thinks of England, or America, or Jamaica.

I photograph a lot of models who are a perfect shape, with perfect tits. They give an impression of being very good in bed, but that is often just a facade. A lot of times, perfect people don't enjoy sex; the plainest Jane could be the best lay in the world and a sex-symbol actress could be lousy. You would expect perfect women to be superb because of the way they look, but a perfect-looking lady isn't necessarily good in bed. She may not be good just because you fancy her. I photograph the Miss World beauty queens in London each year, and the photographers and reporters all compete in trying to lay one of the contestants. It's an ego thing. Beauty queens are the ideal specimens, with perfect shapes. But Miss Germany wasn't very good; according to a certain reporter she just lay back and wanted him to do all the work. The perfect shape is there, but you might as well screw one of those plastic dolls. It's just like sticking it into a hole in the wall.

Part IV

The Oldest Professionals

SHERI

Madam

Sheri has been a madam for fifteen years. She runs one of Nevada's legalized brothels—Sheri's Ranch. She is in her thirties and looks like a brunette Doris Day, with freckles and a ponytail. Over three hundred and fifty girls have worked for Sheri. They rent bedrooms at the ranch on a weekly basis; men pay ten dollars for a straight ten-minute lay, and the price goes up from there according to desired variation.

The ranch is visible for miles around due to a large, lit up "S" and garlands of Christmas tree lights that line the drive. A sign at the end of the drive says "We Take Mastercharge."

Sheri—top madam and ranch owner—is expert at choosing girls with the potential to be good in bed, and in training them to fulfill that potential.

I've seen a lot of girls in my time, and the ones who were good didn't have anything in common about the way they looked, or their characters, or anything. The size of a girl's cunt doesn't matter. She doesn't have to do exercises for the vaginal muscles, or wear special underwear. The only way a girl can be really bad in bed is if she doesn't care, doesn't move. I can't tell if a girl is good by just looking at her. The quickest way I discover that is by the repeat business she gets. You can also tell by the look on the customer's face when he leaves her room. Some girls get picked over and over during the line-up (when the women line up for the men to pick them). I think a woman gets better as she gets older. I don't think a girl's build makes her good in bed or not. Lack of inhibitions is the main thing that makes a woman good.

I choose my girls almost like you would select a secretary. In the same way as a secretary needs to have certain standards before she goes to work in an office girls here need certain standards, like being able to do their hair and makeup properly, before they can work here. First of all, I find out if a girl is going to be good by asking where she has worked before, although it is really much better if a girl hasn't worked anywhere, because then I can train her more quickly. When she arrives, she has to learn the practicalities: the rules and the price list. The girls get five dollars for extra positions—five dollars for each one. (Some girls are better on the bottom, some on top.)

I get one of the older girls to show the T.O.'s (we call them turn-outs) how to go behind a customer and check for disease, and how to persuade him to pay more money. Girls always need hints about how to get more money from a customer, how to sense his moods. Actual technique hints depend on the girl's individual style, because each girl's style is different. On quiet nights, the girls sit around and discuss the men, and the new T.O.'s ask for tips.

However, there are certain tricks we *do* teach the girls—like how to give blowjobs. We have a special jar of pickles and we teach girls on that (the pickles, not the jar). They start by thinking that a blow job is just going up and down a man's cock, but it is also tongue movements, especially at the back of the cock, where the cord is. Put the warmth of your tongue on that, and you have got the man.

There are other hints that girls give each other in this profession. Some men deliberately avoid coming, because they want extra time, more than their money's worth. One of our girls had a man like that the other day, so just at the time she knew he was ready to come, but realized he was stopping himself, she stuck her finger up his ass, which made him come right away.

Every wife wonders what her husband pays for when he pays for sex (90 percent of our customers are married). One of the reasons a man comes here is because there is not going to be any involvement or complications. He is just going to get laid, but the girls are also part mother, part sister, and part psychologist, and every man who comes here has to be made to feel that he is the greatest lover, the most important man in the world, no matter how many other men a girl has had that day.

Of course, the girls do have to fake some things. Although we do have some bisexual girls here who get into threesomes, straight girls don't usually like them. So now and again we give shows when we fake it. But the main thing about the girls here is that they are prepared to do anything; they are not afraid of anything and they will do everything to give a man variety. Many wives are petrified to give blowjobs, or else they are scared to let a man go down on them because they think it is dirty. Lots of men also come here to go down on our girls, or else learn how to. (We teach them by putting whipped cream on our cunts and letting them lick it off.)

What advice would I give to the average woman who wants to be good in bed? To have patience with her man, and to try different things together. I wouldn't advise her to do everything he asks, if she doesn't want to, but I think it helps if she is prepared to try something at least once.

STAR

Novice Hooker

Star is a twenty-three-year-old new "turn-out" at Sheri's Ranch. She has already been married four times. She is Swedish, tall and thin, with long blonde hair. While I was at Sheri's Ranch, the girls had company, and a line-up was held. Ten girls were looked over by three men. "Ladies, will you please rise?" said the madam. "Gentlemen, these are the ladies." Star was the first girl to be chosen.

I expect to be a hooker for the rest of my life and get better and better in bed. We all get on very well here. When I was at college we didn't get on nearly as well, and I am learning a lot from the other girls. The young men go for me in the line-ups. I baby the gentlemen and make them feel the greatest, that everything they do turns me on. I go crazy about them. I talk all the time that relaxes them, but I also massage the men first. Sex is 80 percent mental. If your head is not there, then nothing else is. Before I start with a man, we talk about what he likes and what he wants to do. I don't start with a set idea of what I am going to do.

Faking is about 90 percent. I tell each man everything that he wants to hear. That he has the biggest cock, that you don't like big ones if his is small. They all believe me, because they come back for more. Being good in bed depends on your experience and theirs, and who they have been to bed with before you.

Another thing I do to be good is to feather-tickle them all over with my tongue. Then I suck them off with a mouth full of hot water, followed by ice. (I call that the hot and cold running blondes.) I also suck them off with a mouth full of toothpaste. One thing I refuse to have, though, is anal sex. I have never tried it, and I don't want to. One girl was practically a legend in Nevada. They called her "Three-way Pat." She had had anal sex so often that her entire system was ruined. I also don't really like to lick a guy all the way. I don't ever let a man come in my mouth. I would never swallow come, and I always take a towel to bed. I have been scared to ask men to give me head in my private life. Some guys think that what they are offering—their cocks—is so great that you are mad to ask for more. In the end I eventually *do* ask them, but still, I always hope that men are seeing me for more than sex.

I've never worked in the streets, and I've never been to prison. I hate the idea of not having protection. I like being here, being shut away from the world. I can feel needed this way, because the guys are coming to me. I don't have to hunt for them. They *need* me. That also makes a woman good: the need to be needed.

ICEBERG SLIM
Ex-Pimp

Iceberg Slim was a pimp for over five hundred women, and is the author of the book Pimp *and many others. When I phoned, a deep voice said, "Hello, this is Iceberg, Iceberg Slim." My blood curdled and I nearly canceled the interview, except that I didn't dare. Iceberg greeted me with a handshake outside his house, then took me inside to a decidedly domestic tea with his wife and four children.*

I could never tell if a woman was going to be good in bed until she performed with me. I've known whores who were the ultimate projection of exciting sex, only to discover that they were *not* good in bed. I could never go on assumptions about a whore's performance in bed, because she might end up not making money, which would lead to the worst possible confrontation: between a pimp and a job.

Pimps are asexual. I was in it for the money and not the sex. When you have a stable of twenty girls working for you, you are in trouble if you are into being a superstud. Career pimps, as I was, try to preserve themselves, to conserve their energy. I always appeared very sour, otherwise whores got you in the end. When a pimp was hooked on a whore, we would say, "He has got that bitch's scent up his nose." The essence of the woman got tied up inside their brains, weakening them.

But whores are better in bed than most women. The sexual peak is prior to menopause for most women, the golden age for a woman to be good in bed. But that age is less marketable than youth. Whores are good for acrobatics and slavish devotion—they make the best mechanics. When I say slavish devotion, a whore won't *really* do anything, but she still leaves you with the impression that she has done everything—because whores use their hands, their feet, their voices—they are like quicksilver. They needed to be, because my whores worked eighteen hours a day, and had to bring back $100 a day, even in the thirties.

I like a woman to come to me bringing a reputation for wicked eroticism. Not that she is a pushover, but that she is always free (unlike a whore) to choose whoever she goes to bed with, and that no one forces her or owns her. There is a kind of choreography of sex that matters. Some women, after they have had sex with you for about the third time, have the aptitude to mesh with you. Everything is fluid as you move her through the various sexual positions with the pressure of your fingertips, or even the voice. She flows with you.

Erotic tastebuds also make a woman good in bed, when a woman knows what you want without being told, almost by witchcraft. Also, power in bed is very important: a crossbow back, lots of strength, so that you know when you have taken her to the peak, it will be drama the moment you push her off.

I don't think a woman is less good in bed if she takes a long time to come. I am suspicious of a woman whose furnace you can set ablaze immediately, because sometimes she is faking, or is a nymphomaniac and then you can never hope to satisfy her. Some women are very silent in bed, but I think that the best women are always those who carry on an erotic conversation, a reportage of what they are doing while you are in bed. That is important for the man who really considers himself a great lover, because the woman heightens his glorious self-image by reporting along the way. A woman can also create a good self-image for herself by thinking of herself as an assassin, a killer in bed, with the destruction of the man her ultimate goal.

I've never forced a woman to do anything in bed. Women always did what I wanted anyway—they were all good partners and wanted to please me. I am not talking about whores—they try to tire pimps out with fellatio. They do it all the time, even in the car—and they swallow (it kills oral sex if a woman refuses to swallow).

Physical build doesn't make a woman better in bed, just different. Thin women are more susceptible to choreography, more fluidity, but plump women also compete in their own way, with warmth and softness. Chemistry has a lot to do with what makes a woman good in bed. It is produced when two psyches meet and their oils, their fluids, coalesce; that is what produces good sex.

MARY
Hollywood Hooker

Mary is a twenty-year-old Hollywood hooker who works from her apartment. She wears see-through blouses and an Afro hairstyle. Mary started at sixteen, trading sex for drugs. Now she takes ten customers a week, charging up to $50 a session.

I know that I am good in bed. I've worked in parlors and men have always followed me, so I can't be doing that much wrong. I need to be good and please a man, otherwise he won't ever come back to me. The first thing I do to be good is ask a man what makes him happy, what he wants in bed. Some men are shocked, or they don't know what to do except fuck, but they finally tell me what they want.

I don't really know if I do anything special in bed. I know the main thing is to help men act out their fantasies. Men pay to come to me because I will do things their wives won't do (like give head), and act out any fantasy they ask for. Men have weird fantasies, so I have done strange things.

Once I had a man who wanted me to let him screw me in the sink, full of dishwater and bubbles. I was a bit embarrassed, he was standing on a chair and leaning on the side of the sink and I was sitting astride in it, with all the bubbles and dishwater. That happened because he had watched his wife wash up and had fantasized about throwing her in the dishwater and fucking her. He never dared actually to do that to her, but he could to me—which makes me good.

But, in fact, you don't have to do what a man wants every time. I never let men beat me, and I won't beat them with a leather strap, only a wet towel, because it never leaves welts. I also never have sex with someone and afterwards give him head. The main thing, though, is that I can't stand anyone coming in my mouth. I hate it. Even though I am getting paid, I tell men straight away that I won't do it. No one has ever asked me for his money back or has ever said that I was not good in bed because I didn't let him come in my mouth. You can't be good in bed if you hate what you are doing.

Men still want you to think that they are the greatest in bed, even though they are just paying to go to bed with you. You have to make them believe that they are really giving you a treat and act as if you are enjoying it. Even if a man's prick is tiny, I still say things like, "Oh, it hurts." Then, if they say it may not be big enough for me, I tell them it is beautiful, that it is just the right size for me. They tell you that they *know* it is really small—their wives have told them so. Never mind if you can't even feel it when they are fucking you, you still have to say, "Oh, it is lovely. It is the average size." Once I had a man who had elephantiasis of the balls. They were enlarged, but I still did everything I could not to make him feel insecure.

Last summer, I did really well. I went to Vegas for five days and made $1,200. I stayed at the Dunes and then at the MGM Grand. No one bothered me, even thought it is illegal to be a hooker in Vegas. I was approached and asked to be a house girl at Caesar's Palace. I was told that I would get 60 percent of everything that I made. I don't know how the men who asked knew that I would be good in bed, (because I don't think you can tell by looking). No one tried me out, they just said they liked the way I looked, dressed, and walked. (I was very conservative and clean-cut, rather like a college girl.) In Vegas you have to look like a lady or else you get busted.

One man in Las Vegas gave me $250 just for an hour. He was a gynecologist, about forty-five, and I gave him a bit of head and just balled. I suppose wives might wonder what I did for all that money that *they* can't do. The answer has nothing to do with looks; it's difficult to explain. You might be the most beautiful girl in the world, but just lie there and not know what to do. I have been to orgies and watched women lie still and scream, but still not do anything.

If a man told me he would give me $500 to be extra good, I would be sugar and honey and keep telling him that he was fantastic. I know I am not perfect, but I know how to be good in bed. A lot of men get turned on if you tighten your muscles while they are screwing you—not just when they come—especially if you do it really quickly. Then I also make very quick strokes. Of course I fake a lot, all the noises and that, but the main thing to fake is that you are having a relationship with the man you are in bed with, even though all the time he is just *paying* to fuck you. Pretending you have a relationship is what makes a woman good in bed, and then men always come back for more.

GINA

Nevada Hooker

Gina is the hooker who makes the most money at Sheri's Ranch. New girls are trained in the bedroom next to Gina. They listen through the wall to what she says to her customers, and when the new girls get their own customers, they follow Gina's cues. Gina is in her late thirties, a red-haired version of Mae West, Amazon-like, with broad shoulders. She has had so many men she's lost count.

When men choose a woman here, they choose their fantasy woman. I recognize the men who will pick me the minute they walk in. Professional, older. They pick me because they think they can handle me in bed, because they are so great.

I am good because I talk to the men. I constantly compliment a man. As soon as he walks into my room I tell him I am glad that he is visiting me. Once I have examined him I tell him to lie down and then I say, "Gee, you dress nicely." Then a few minutes later I say, "Gee, you smell good." Then I tell him how great he looks from the chest down. Most of the sexual act is talk. I don't care what size a man's prick is, I still tell him it is the greatest I have ever had. "Gee, it's big. God it's great." Even if the man's prick is a little bit above average, I say, "My God, what a weapon. Take it easy, slowly, I love it." They hardly last long at all.

Some men like me to talk dirty as well. Of all the things, I refuse anal sex, but then not many men want it. Seventy percent of wives don't give oral sex, so I do a lot of that. I use concentrated mouthwash on the tip of my tongue, or else creme de menthe and ice, or warm water. I put a teaspoonful in my mouth and let it dribble all over their pricks, then I use a little piece of ice. Then I do an all-over French licking. I do round the world with that. I nibble their rear ends, then I go in gently, as if I am screwing up their backsides with my tongue, not all the way in, though. I do a lot around the rim, and then down their legs. I give a massage and also run my fingertips lightly all over the man's body.

Usually I get on top of them, because I have big tits and men like to watch. Some men like to push your legs over your head, but I try not to let them, as it can hurt the cervix if you fuck as often as I do. I like to be on top doing it to them; then I can control the fucking.

I have gotten better in bed as I have gotten older. I know how to treat a man because I am experienced. If a virgin asked me how to be good, I would tell her that the main thing is to make the man feel wanted and needed. I would also show her how to give head, on a banana, and not to bite.

Men don't come to me just for sex. They come to be treated nice and to get away from all the bitching at home. When they come here, their ideal woman has to be romantic, has to smell good, to look good, and to be good, otherwise they would stay at home.

There is a difference between the sex I have here and the sex I have with someone I love. I never swallow come anywhere. I take it all in, but I don't swallow it, I just spit it into a handkerchief. When I love a man I do the same physical things as for a customer, except that I kiss him, and I never kiss a customer. I give the man I love sex and emotion, but I don't ever come with fucking. I never have, just with head. I don't think that makes me less good in bed. I would rather please a man than be pleased. It excites me when men get turned on.

I regard my life at Sheri's Ranch as a business, but the men don't know that. The main thing is that I find company here. I like my work, and every man who walks through this door is company for me. There is something nice about every one of them. You see, I loved someone who died, and I am here because I need company. And the men who come here also need company, so we are good in bed for each other.

BIBA

Beverly Hills Call Girl

Biba operates as a call girl from her Beverly Hills apartment. She looks like Jane Fonda in Klute. *She is red-headed, animated, and exaggeratedly elegant.*

I like sex, and you have to like sex to be good in bed. I have fun, and I have orgasms with the guys I see professionally. When a new guy walks through this door, it's really exciting and interesting for me because I wonder what his trip is going to be—what he's going to ask me to do. Men expect all kinds of things, and I have some very interesting clients. Helping live out their fantasies and being adaptive to clients is one of the things that make me good in bed. A guy feels safe about telling a professional his fantasies. He is paying for special treatment he can't get from his wife or his girlfriend, so he tells a call girl what he wants her to do.

I see this one guy who is a very famous tennis player, very handsome, and really sweet. But he told me that he couldn't ask his girlfriends to do what he asks me because they would reject him or laugh at him. So when he sees me, he wants me to tie him up; the room has to be dark, I can't talk, there can't be any music. You see, he has a leg and foot fetish. I just lie on the bed and I rub my legs on his cheek and he strokes my legs with his hands very, very gently. His eyes are closed and he is just tripping, and if I put my foot in his face, he has an orgasm. The first time I did that to him, tears were streaming down his face, he was so happy.

I have another client who is a stockbroker and looks like a sweet, all-American boy next door. When he comes here, he likes to crawl on his hands and knees. Then I tie a cord around his cock and lead him around the floor. I wear either boots or black high-heel shoes, my black fishnet stockings, and a lacy black bra. Then I order him to lick my shoes, lick my toes, lick my feet. He loves that. He loves me to sit on his face and smother him with my buttocks. He won't even let me brace myself, and I have to put all my weight on his face. That is not hard work. If I want him to fuck me, then I have him fuck me. If I want him to jack off, then I have him jack off—I order him to. Everything is all right so long as I *order* him to do it.

Other guys like me to pretend to be a little girl. One guy had me fly to Sacramento, and I had to wear a little dress and white cotton panties underneath. He told me about his first sexual experience, which he had when he and the girl were very young. He was reliving the experience.

Some guys I see have incest fantasies. There's an older man I see. He likes me to act the little girl, and I call him Uncle Jack and he loves it. He calls me on the phone from his Rolls Royce when he's driving down the road and he says, "This is your Uncle Jack. Can I come up and see you?"

I really adapt to the needs of my clients. I care very much about giving them satisfaction so they will come back really happy. I am never judgmental. I never put them down for their fantasies. Sometimes though, it's difficult. I have very few inhibitions left, but once a doctor from Philadelphia offered me a lot of money because he wanted me to pee on him. I was very inhibited about that, but because I am a professional I knew I *had* to do it. So I told the guy to bring me a bottle of champagne, because I needed to be a little bit drunk to be loosened up and able to do it.

But most guys are not that way-out. They want you to pay attention to them, chat to them. They want to have a pretty girl talking to them. They always sense whether the attraction is real or not. You see, I never bullshit clients. I just show them real appreciation, because I really am pleased to see them and I really do enjoy them in bed. So I don't have to say, "Oh you are fantastic," (unless the guy hints that he wants that).

There's a producer I see who told me he met some girl who said his cock was so big and tasted so good. His cock really is just average, but I realized, by what he said, that he needed to be told differently. So if that's what he wants, then that's what I do, and I tell him, "Oh, she was certainly right." Usually, though, I talk very little to my clients in bed, and I don't talk dirty unless the guy asks for it. Otherwise, I am very much the lady in every sense, and I never swear.

I started out by working for Dixie, a madam, and she taught me a lot, and "turned me out." When we met, we just talked and she told me to lose weight, which I did. She also told me not to wear wigs, only to wear real gold jewelry, not tons of make-up, and no false eyelashes. Also, she told me to wear a light perfume and long dresses which look elegant and classy, and are easy to get in and out of—long dresses that you don't have to wear anything underneath.

Dixie didn't tell me anything about technique, but she explained how to cope if a guy gets too rough—you act really sweet and calm. But, anyway, when you work for a madam you have protection, because she is in the other room and the guys know that you can always call her. The only trouble is that a couple of guys have wanted to fuck me really really hard, so I just say, "Honey, not so hard. I'm just a little thing," or else, "Oh, honey, your cock's so big it's hurting me," in a little tiny voice. Dixie told me that when that happens, I should wrap my legs around the man's back and brace myself with my thighs, so even though the guy is really banging on your thigh and not your pussy, he thinks you have wrapped your legs around him to pull him closer to you.

I don't like my tricks to fuck me really hard, but my boyfriend always fucks me really, really hard, and I like that. I keep a real definite separation between my lovers and my tricks. When I'm with my boyfriend in bed, we look in each other's eyes while we make love. I love that. It increases the intensity of the experience. I don't do that with my clients. I don't look into their eyes because I don't want that closeness with a client. My boyfriend and I act out my fantasies. I have masochistic fantasies, and I only act them out with him. Sometimes I have a little bruise on my arm or on my leg, and then the guys who see me professionally say, "Oh, Biba, who did that to you? Oh, how terrible!" and they get really upset.

A lot of guys who see me for business spend all their time eating me. They say, "Biba, if I can make you come, that's important for me." I think eating a woman is the nicest thing a guy can do. I get a customer who comes from San Diego every Friday and brings a little brown bag of all the things he wants to eat out of my pussy: bananas, whipped cream, chocolate-covered cherries and strawberries. When he does that, I have fun; having fun is one of the most important things about being good in bed.

Giving head matters a lot in bed, and also phallic worship. When I am with my Uncle Jack (as the little girl) and we neck for a while on the couch, then I have him unzip his fly and get his cock out, and I get down on my knees and I take his cock and rub it over my cheeks and over my lips and over my eyes. It's like worshipping it; then he knows that I really appreciate it and it's not just a quick blowjob. I swallow a man's come if I know the guy and he doesn't taste bad. Every guy tastes so different. I'm sure women also taste differently as well.

I am just getting better and better in bed. Guys teach me different things, and I have plenty of time and opportunity to experiment. If a woman asked how to be good in bed, I would advise her to ask the man to tell her his fantasy. If she found it difficult to ask, I would advise her to say, "Is there any special way I can please you? What would you like? I'll do anything. Just ask me and I'll do it.''

You should also experiment with a guy's body and how he feels good, and you should change positions with him. You should also get in touch with your own fantasies and your own trips and not be so concerned about just pleasing the man. Allow him to please you, too. Both of you should share your fantasies and what turns you on, then you will both be satisfied. It's not a one-way deal. You should also make love in different kinds of places. I like to do something very trippy. I might make love in front of a mirror, or do it in front of the fireplace, or on the dining room table.

Guys turn on to a woman if she's sweet, feminine, sexy, and really interested in them. (It doesn't matter what she really looks like.) And a woman who wants to be good in bed should never judge the man she is in bed with. In this business I have learned that sex is a very individual thing, that each person wants something different and *is* something different. It doesn't matter what the guy looks like. He can be big and fat, or real old, or real skinny. None of that matters. I suspend all judgments. I just enjoy the men's warmth and just being close to them.

MICHAEL KEARNS

Male Hooker

Michael Kearns, author of The Happy Hustler, *has slept with over three hundred women during his career as a professional hooker.*

Women are made to feel insecure because there are all sorts of silly platitudes about what makes a woman good in bed. If I averaged out the best sexual experiences, they weren't with women who are blonde and twenty. The ideal woman in bed can be anything physically—not always thin or fat, not always tall or small. I can tell how highly sexed a woman is by watching her eat—the sensuousness of holding a glass shows if the woman is good, if she handles it as if she was handling a cock. You get a whole feeling of rhythm, which is important; I can sometimes even tell if a woman is good on the phone by the rhythm, the intensity of her voice.

I can always tell if a woman is good in bed by looking into her eyes, or at her mouth. I really think eyes and mouths have a lot to do with being good in bed. Marilyn Monroe looked as if she was very good—she had the right mouth—but I never went to bed with her, so I am not certain. Perhaps she wasn't good at all, just because she projected it so strongly. The projection of sex often means that the woman can be a flop in bed. There are so many sex goddesses who have flopped in the bedroom, so instead, they have sex with the whole world.

I don't think a woman is very good in bed if she *thinks* about being good while she is having sex. There has to be some spontaneity. The inhibitions do lessen after a certain amount of experience, or when a woman gets involved in an emotional attachment which makes her feel free and uninhibited. The ideal sexual situation is the freedom to do whatever you want in bed.

A lot of women come to me because they have insecurities, the worst being oral sex; at thirty-five they are doing it for the first time. (Some people, even today, still think that sex exists just to have children.) Other women were housewives and used my services because they wanted something different and were afraid to ask for it. Demands need to be made in bed, but a lot of women don't know how to make demands—they are so scared of not being thought good.

I am really a feminist. I think the woman has felt at a gut level that she should not have a sexual self or explore. Women's idea of sex used to be passive and to do whatever the man asks. I disagree with that. On any level, not just physical, it is pointless to have a relationship with someone who only wants to please you. What I would like to say to all women is, "Get rid of stereotypes, forget all that masculine and feminine labeling." I am not saying that we should reverse roles, but that each individual has the capacity to relate or interrelate in many different ways—some masculine and some feminine. I don't think that softness in a man should be despised, or toughness in a woman condemned.

I like older women, assertive women—not that I like whips and chains, but I do like a woman who does what she wants in bed. I think what makes a woman good is being able to give and take—she should never be just the giver.

Of course, there are some women who are bad in bed because they are scared and they are very submissive, or they are lazy and don't move. It's easy to just lie there. But a woman isn't bad if she takes a long time to come. Some men keep asking if the woman has come, but that acts like a stoplight to women; it makes them freeze.

I don't try to judge my partner or say, "Did you come?" or "You were really good." I don't verbalize in bed. But, at the same time, I would never pretend I am the perfect screw, or that because I am six-foot-two, I might be better than someone who is five-foot-two. Society has shoved down our throats everything that we are supposed to be, so that you feel that if you don't look like someone in a commercial, you shouldn't have sex.

The trouble is that everyone is scared—and sexually scared of not being perfect, but no one is perfect in bed; everyone is different—sexually, emotionally, intellectually, physically.

No matter how similar we may *seem,* there is always something different. Everyone should hold fast to that. Every single woman I have been with has been totally different from moment to moment, from day to day, from hour to hour. In the course of intercourse, our moods change, our fantasies change. No two people are alike. There is no good in bed or bad in bed, just different.

I know that "Are you good in bed?" will still be a terrible question for women to answer. I only hope that it will now become an equally terrible question for men to ask. I don't believe this book has revealed any formula for what makes a woman good in bed, but has just proved that none exists.

The book has had great personal significance for me, but since I wanted to have a perspective on its general significance, I gave the manuscript to a leading psychologist for his comments:

"This book reflects the human reality behind the sex manuals, so that instead of supersex, we have human sex.

"It gets away from all formulas, humanizing that great destructive force in sexual emancipation: the depersonalization of sex. You interviewed people who symbolize being good in bed, and they responded as human beings, showing the great variety, the unexpectedness, the varied approaches and desires of people.

"If all those you appealed to had said the same thing, had given *the* formula for being good in bed, then the ordinary person, falling short of that formula, would have felt diminished.

"I would hope that the book will make everyone feel better by removing the feeling 'I am no good in bed because I don't meet an absolute,' as I think you have abolished the absolute by getting away from formulas, showing the infinite variety of the possible.

"It shows that being good isn't one thing, but a whole range of things; therefore we can all join in because 'little me' may be good in bed, too.

"I hope the book will help people, reassure them, giving them confidence and expectation in their own sexual lives and in their potentially for greater sexual happiness."

P.S. on GIB*

*good in bed

Frank Sinatra once said that all lady journalists are hookers. Some people seem to believe him, so it was hardly surprising that the men I met while writing this book continually misinterpreted me, acting as if I had invented a novel way of approaching attractive men.

Men I met for the first time expected me to be instantly available; and men I was available to expected me to be instantly incredible. Men I knew well talked to me less and seemed to feel they had something to prove. They would discuss their prowess and hint that they expected a high rating. Sometimes it seemed as though I was taking the book to bed with me, which occasionally obscured and even destroyed my relationships.

Over and over men would say to me, "I have explained what makes a woman good—now tell me what you think makes a man good." Sometimes men I found unattractive asked me this. Then I answered, "The subtlety of his initial approach to me," discouraging them by giving the impression that the game was over, or that beginning it required an intricate approach of which they were incapable. Sometimes men I did find attractive asked me that question.

I knew that there was a way of answering, but I also knew that it would be far too complex and multi-dimensional for one sentence. Finally I decided that the subject required further investigation and merited another adventure—another book.